MW01591068

Agents of uncertainty

Consciousness Literature the & Arts 31

General Editor:
Daniel Meyer-Dinkgräfe

Editorial Board:
Anna Bonshek, Per Brask, John Danvers,
William S. Haney II, Amy Ione,
Michael Mangan, Arthur Versluis,
Christopher Webster, Ralph Yarrow

Agents of uncertainty
mysticism, scepticism, Buddhism, art and poetry

John Danvers

Amsterdam - New York, NY 2012

Cover illustration by John Danvers ©.

Cover design by Aart Jan Bergshoeff

The paper on which this book is printed meets the requirements of "ISO 9706:1994, Information and documentation - Paper for documents - Requirements for permanence".

ISBN: 978-90-420-3512-6
ISSN: 1573-2193
E-Book ISBN: 978-94-012-0787-4
E-book ISSN: 1879-6044
© Editions Rodopi B.V., Amsterdam - New York, NY 2012
Printed in the Netherlands

Printed by Printforce, the Netherlands

Contents

Illustrations

*All the drawings, collages or photographs are made by the author.
They are intended as a visual counterpoint to the text.*

Page

Preface

Basil Girbau, the hermit of
Montserrat, once said:

"You are here. What more do you want?
You breathe. Your heart beats.
What matters yesterday?
What matters tomorrow?
You are here.
So laugh, laugh until you burst.
You have what is essential.
You don't need more or less".
(Girbau 2003)

A place to start, setting the scene...

This book has grown out of what seemed, for a time, to be two separate or divergent lines of enquiry. On the one hand, an interest in what can be seen as a sceptical counter-tradition to the system-building mainstream of Western philosophical ideas. On the other, an interest in the cluster of perceptions, ideas and values referred to as mysticism. My initial readings in these fields of enquiry suggested that they were in mutual opposition, or at least that there was a profound tension and discord between them. However, I have come to realise that there is a surprising concordance in methods and aims espoused by many mystics and sceptics. In a sense mysticism is a realisation of, or arises from, a deep scepticism about all the statements, doings and speculations of human beings, while the questioning of appearances, ideas and assertions by sceptics is undertaken in order to achieve a state of imperturbability (*ataraxia*), bliss or peace of mind – which is something to which many mystics would, and do, aspire.

It is this intertwining of aspirations, methods, insights and achievements that I explore in various ways in the following chapters. Undoubtedly the social and cultural contexts within which mystics and sceptics have lived differ greatly from place to place and time to time.

While scepticism tends to be associated with atheism, mysticism is usually considered as a particular manifestation of theistic religious experience. However, even this apparently obvious distinction is itself questionable when account is taken of the many mystics who reside within non-theistic religions, for example, Daoism and Buddhism, and those within a theistic tradition who mount a critique of many aspects of that tradition. Likewise, there are many examples of sceptical thinkers who nonetheless seem to practice a particular religion and articulate their thoughts in religious, often theistic, terms – for instance, Montaigne and Pascal.

Many forms of scepticism and mysticism can also be seen as having common opponents or antitheses. While sceptics argue against most kinds of dogmatism and attachment to fixed ideas of truth or justified belief, many mystics espouse a deep suspicion of the reliability of believing in appearances and anthropocentric values. Mystical practices are often concerned with developing disciplines of doubt in order to re-focus or de-centre the individual in relation to a transcendent order or a radically revised mode of being-in-the-world. In these cases, at least, dogmatism can be seen as the antithesis of mysticism, as it is of the sceptical method. Mystics and sceptics are "free" thinkers in the sense that they are not attached, or aspire not to be attached, to appearances, essences, definitions, categories, fixed positions or ideas. Mystics, sceptics, artists and poets tread paths of uncertainty toward states of equanimity and inner peace. They endeavour to tread a middle path between all opinions, judgements and certainties. They work towards being free of attachment to dogmas.

My aim in the following pages is firstly to explore some of the ideas and practices articulated by mystics and sceptics, and secondly to show how some artists and poets enact and, at times, question these ideas and practices in their work.

Mysticism, language *and* experience

In the past thirty to forty years there has been a marked change in the way that mysticism is discussed, reflecting changes in the methods and discourses of theology, cultural theory and philosophy. This change involves a move away from the analysis of, or even acceptance of, direct experience, and towards an investigation into the language of mysticism – a shift of focus from modes of experience to modes of mediation. In the following pages I have taken account of this shift, making use of a number of recent studies that suggest interesting affinities and overlaps between mysticism, scepticism, poetics and art.

I hope that the approach I have taken will shed a fresh light on these exciting fields of being, knowing and doing – fields that I explore as bodies of ideas and values enacted in a variety of scholarly, artistic and poetic practices which demonstrate some of the ways in which human life can be lived and experience.

To the reader

This book arises from my own experiences, erratic readings and mis-readings in many fields. I have no formal training in philosophy and make no special claims to knowledge in any field. As a practising artist, writer and teacher I have pursued particular interests in art practice and theory, aesthetics, poetry and poetics, and in the history of ideas. As a wayward practitioner of *zazen* and mindfulness I have made an unsystematic study of aspects of Buddhism, Daoism and Asian culture. If I was pushed into characterising my own position in as few words as possible I might claim that I am a sceptical Buddhist raised in an ostensibly Christian culture. As such, it is important to point out that the opposite of what I have to say may well be as *true* or useful as what I do say, and is certainly worthy of equal consideration.

I hope that there will be something in the following pages to interest and stimulate both the general and specialist reader.

Acknowledgements

I wish to thank Rodopi for permission to include in a revised form extracts from my earlier book, *Picturing Mind* (2006) – particularly the sections on: *Sunyata* (pages 69-71 in Picturing Mind); The use of *koan*s – a dialectics of absurdity (ibid: 94-96); Heidegger, *Dasein* and kinship (ibid: 161-162); Martin Heidegger – God as an open field of infinite possibility (ibid: 272-276; and Baruch Spinoza. (ibid: 80-83)

I am grateful to the organisers of numerous conferences for the opportunity to explore some of the ideas developed in the following pages – most recently to Jamie Cresswell and Val Stephenson at the Institute of Oriental Philosophy in Taplow. Harry Youtt and Daniel Meyer-Dinkgräfe provided me with astute and helpful editorial advice – for which I am very grateful. I am also indebted to my students, past and present, for so many stimulating questions and ideas. And special thanks to Charles for his friendship, wisdom, and wit.

For Philippa, Joanna, Tom and Jenny

Introduction

The goal of composition, is "not to reach conclusion
but to keep our exposure to what we do not know."
– the American poet, Robert Duncan.
(Duncan 2010)

The book as a narrative of open-ended enquiry

This book comprises a gathering of notes, narratives, ideas and images
that trace various strands of enquiry. In weaving together these strands
of thought I have constructed what might be considered to be an erratic or ragged argument – indeed it may not constitute an argument at
all in the usual sense of making a case for a particular point of view. It
may be more accurately described as a collage or *Florilegium* – an
accretion of ideas and suggestions or an unfolding of possibilities. As
an open-ended process of enquiry it can yield no definitive answers,
final conclusions or certainties. This mode of organisation seems to
me to most closely reflect or embody what goes on in this mind that I
provisionally, and perhaps mistakenly, consider to be my own.

Interwoven into the explicatory discourse of the book is another strand
of writing that approaches mysticism and scepticism from a more
poetic perspective. This strand includes a series of *Observations* –
descriptions or evocations of the sensory field within which I exist and
write – the quotidian ground out of which ideas and images arise in
the imagination. It seems important as I think, reflect and write, to
acknowledge that these activities are manifestations of an embodied
mind in a particular place – on *this* chair, in *this* room, at *this* time –
and that they are manifestations of a mind that is open and indeterminate, the hub of an ever-changing network of relationships.

An image comes into view that may be useful: the embodied mind is
like a small stream into which other rivulets flow from all directions
and which in turn flows into a larger river. The stream is full of currents of images, ideas, stories, memories and feelings that are always
in motion, never still. These currents are produced by the interactions

between whatever flows into the stream and the terrain through which it runs. The surface of the stream also reflects everything that surrounds it. The stream is translucent and often transparent. There is no definite edge or boundary to it and who can say who owns the currents which flow through it or who can know everything that goes on within it. The stream is pulled by the gravity of time, flowing inexorably to the sea. It is both unique *and* inseparable from everything that surrounds it.

As I gaze out of the window from where I sit to write these notes, I see hawthorn blossoms like constellations of stars set against the shadows of taller trees. I see the delicate fronds of mimosa bending in the light breeze coming in from the estuary – a silvered gash in the blue horizon. All around I hear the cooing of wood pigeons, the eloquent song of blackbirds and the distant murmur of the city in the valley below. Thoughts arise for a moment only to fade and return once more into the flow of sights and sounds. These sensations and scattered thoughts constitute the shifting focus of attention as I write and give shape to the flux of being. It is this shifting shimmering field that puzzles, excites and challenges all of us as we live our lives, and it is this field of being that many mystics and sceptics have sought to fathom and explore. Their writings map the course of journeys made, and explain as far as they are able how they travelled and what they experienced along the way.

Brief outline

What follows is organised into seven parts. In Part I I describe and discuss various currents of thought and modes of practice within mysticism. Reference is made to Thomas Merton, Martin Heidegger, Meister Eckhart, Jacob Boehme, Baruch Spinoza and Teresa of Avila. Connections are also made between the ideas of these writers on mysticism with the process-based philosophy of John Dewey and the work of a number of poets, including T.S. Eliot, Charles Tomlinson and Kathleen Jamie. Part II explores some of the ideas and issues surrounding mysticism and language, with particular reference to aspects of postmodern theology and critical theory – including the work of Don Cupitt, Jacques Derrida, Simone Weil, Roland Barthes and Jean-

Luc Marion. The poetry of R.S. Thomas is discussed in relation to the themes of transcendence and the relative presence and absence of God.

Part III is devoted to a description and discussion of the ideas and methods manifested within various strands of scepticism. The writings of Sextus Empiricus, Michel de Montaigne and David Hume are considered in relation to the early Greek sceptics. Particular reference is made to the ways in which some writers argue for compatibility between Christian belief and sceptical modes of thinking. The work of Samuel Beckett is briefly discussed as an example of sceptical enquiry used to strip away cant, hubris and habits of belief – a process that can be seen as both discomforting and liberating. Part IV focuses on aspects of Buddhist thought and practice, discussed in relation to both mysticism and scepticism. Key concepts such as *sunyata* (absence of self-existence) and interdependence are discussed alongside the practice of mindfulness and *zazen* (sitting meditation). The work of a number of Buddhist writers is considered, including: Dogen, Hakuin and Stephen Batchelor. A brief introduction to Daoist thought follows, opening up threads of connection between Daoist ideas, Buddhism and scepticism.

Part V introduces the idea of the *contrarium* and a brief discussion of the dialectics of Roland Barthes, Theodor Adorno, G.K. Chesterton and others. Ideas about how to make sense of the competing demands of many, very different, even incompatible, truths and opinions, are explored in relation to these writers and to the Jain tradition in Indian philosophy. Part VI is devoted to a consideration of the role art and poetry can play in facing up to the contingencies of everyday life – particularly how artists and poets can act as agents of uncertainty, transforming what might seem to be a negative fear of change and uncertainty into a positive acceptance and excitement. Examples discussed include: Marina Abramovic, John Cage, Charles Wright, Bill Viola and W.S Merwin. Part VII includes a brief note about my own experience of *zazen* practice and a drawing together of many of the threads of the book – not with any sense of summation or completion, but as one possible reading of all that has gone before.

Part I

Mysticism

"It is said of Abbot Agatho that for three years
he carried a stone in his mouth
until he learned to be silent".
(in Merton 1970: 30

"A certain elder said: apply yourself to silence,
have no vain thoughts and be intent in your meditation".
(ibid: 47)

Introduction – what is mysticism?

I use the term *mysticism* to refer to a very diverse set of ideas and practices described in a heterogeneous body of writings and recorded oral statements, centred on distinctive beliefs about being, ideas about living, and methods of attaining particular states of awareness of the flux of living – and the vocabularies and discourses that are used to describe and analyse such states. In this chapter I draw on the writings of a wide range of mystics and on commentaries by other authors who have addressed different aspects of mysticism; these include: Teresa of Avila, Jacob Boehme, the anonymous author of *The Cloud of Unknowing*, Meister Eckhart, Martin Heidegger, Thomas Merton, T.S. Eliot and Baruch Spinoza. I have focused on those aspects of mysticism which support my contention that there are profound similarities in ideas, intentions and methods in the practices and writings of mystics and sceptics. There are, of course, many differences between the two fields but I do not intend to address these in this text – the extant literature already provides ample evidence of a widespread belief in the dissimilarities between mysticism and scepticism, to the extent that they are often considered as being antithetical to each other.

The literature of mysticism, primary and secondary, is punctuated with many attempts to define the term. I have discussed some of these definitions in a previous book (Danvers 2006: 261-276) and I will not revisit the issue here.

NB. In the following pages I use the term "self" on many occasions. In the main I distinguish between two forms or views of the self: the unitary, ego-centred, conventional self – sometimes referred to as the Cartesian self – a view of the self as being relatively fixed and clearly bounded with a distinct essence or core (sometimes also referred to as a soul); and, an alternative view of the self as a porous, permeable process – open to continual change, construction and revision – the relational self. I hope by the end of the book it will become reasonably clear what is meant by these two versions of the self, how different they are and the implications of these differences for how we think about human being.

Being here

At the heart of mysticism lies something apparently very simple: the mystery, wonder and sheer good fortune of being alive. Mystics of every tradition and time are fascinated by, surprised at, and deeply grateful for, the fact of being here. While the rest of humanity may take this fact for granted, letting it settle into the background of their lives, except in extremis, mystics have it in mind most of the time. They try to live, think and feel through this great mystery, using the disciplines and tools available to them. For mystics, being here, being conscious, is never a given, an assumption, it is always something edged with uncertainty and ineffability. Something to be investigated through thought and feeling, something to be weighed and tested, something to be attended to with great intensity and to be condensed into poetry and imagery, words and signs.

As we shall see, in a curiously similar way, sceptics are also puzzled by existence, curious as to what it is to be here. Sceptics take nothing for granted, there is an element of doubt about everything, a sense of uncertainty as to what is, a recognition that what *is* can never be defined, let alone be contained or accurately mapped by human discourse or description. There is always something ungraspable and irreducible about the way things are, something always out of reach of human understanding. No wonder many mystics and sceptics manifest a shared sense of wonder, humility and open-minded inquisitiveness about existence.

These aspects of mysticism, the awareness of being here and the sense of wonder and gratitude at being here, are to me of primary importance. Being fully conscious of *this* life, seems, to me at least, to precede and outshine any awareness of, or belief in, a transcendent reality. Awakening to the flux of being *here* is more important than any desire for, or belief in, being *there*, being somewhere else.

I do not know whether there is a transcendent reality outside of, or beyond, the reality I apprehend with my senses. Cogent and persuasive arguments can be made both for and against such beliefs. There are those who argue from a broadly materialist perspective that reality consists of what can be perceived by the senses and therefore there is no alternative absolute, ideal or transcendent reality. There are those who reasonably claim that the senses can often mislead us and give rise to mistaken beliefs and ideas. There are also those who agree that reality consists of what can be perceived but that our perceptual apparatus includes more than just the traditional five senses. If we add to these senses other modes of perception manifested within intuitive, contemplative and ecstatic states, then even the perceptualist argument can be marshalled in support of a belief in realities that transcend or ground the material world.

Many would also claim that the notion of the "material world" is itself ambiguous and open to interrogation – for sub-atomic and quantum physics proposes, and possibly provides evidence for, a radical re-appraisal of what we mean by materiality and substance. The appearance of substance may obscure a much less tangible state of affairs in which process, energy and perpetual change characterise what is actually happening within objects and substances. To claim dogmatically that there is only one solid, material and tangible reality seems to me to be as unreasonable as to claim, with certainty, that the material world is an illusion – a false reality of appearances behind, or beyond, which exists a transcendent or absolute reality.

While many, if not most, studies of mysticism portray the mystic as someone seeking transcendence, aspiring to knowledge and awareness of a transcendent order – be it *God, ground of being* or *pure consciousness* – I would like to argue for a different emphasis in the way we think about mysticism, focusing particularly on the different ways in which mystics engage with the reality of this life, rather than with a reality that may lie beyond this life (whether expressed in terms of "heaven", the "supernatural" or an "after-life"). While the latter approach emphasises ideas of perfection, the absolute and eternity, the former emphasises experiences of contingency, impermanence and change.

So I come back to the awareness of being alive, being here, being conscious. Being here seems to me to be more than enough to awaken to, to be grateful for and to celebrate. This awareness is itself worthy of wonder, joy and ecstasy, and, in my view, this awareness and its associated feelings and ideas seem to characterise the writings and other modes of expression of many mystics and sceptics. It can be argued that this awareness is integral to *most* mystical traditions, whereas the idea that the goal of mysticism is to enter a transcendent realm or absolute reality only applies to some of them. The fact that this primary awareness is itself mysterious and complex gives rise to the many different ways in which being alive is signified and manifested in the arts and sciences – for the sciences have also turned their attention to the study of consciousness and to the question, what is it to be alive, to be conscious, and to the related question of what is mind?

Of course we may argue, as Chuang-tzu and Jorge-Luis Borges amongst others have argued, that we are ourselves only the dreams or imaginings of some other being and that our consciousness is subsumed within, or is a manifestation of, a greater consciousness. This idea is given credence in some currents of religious and philosophical thinking and is very resistant to refutation. The belief that we are only a small part of a universal mind is advocated by Hindu practitioners, Emersonian transcendentalists, Spinoza and others. However, in a sense this belief does nothing to change, let alone diminish, our experience of attending to the pulse of existence as it arises in our consciousness.

However doubtful one may be about the validity of a belief in transcendence, it is important to acknowledge some of the valuable consequences of such a belief. For instance, while the pursuit of transcendence can be considered as a desire to escape mundane quotidian existence – to be somewhere else – it can also be seen as a recognition that things exist outside the narrow boundaries of the unitary self. Indeed a belief in an essential ego-centred self almost necessitates a belief in a transcendent "other", outside of or separate from the self. Thus it becomes important to try to step outside the limitations and frame of reference of the ego/self, and in so doing, to recognise that the universe does not circulate around the individual human being and may not be a projection of human consciousness. This aspect of a belief in a transcendent otherness can lead to humility and compassion when engaging with others and with the universe as other, even though it may also lead to a marginalisation or undervaluing of *this* life.

The awareness of being alive can be conceptualised in many different ways: as flow and change – the flux of living; as a timeless state of being present in the here and now; as a state of silence, quietness, absence and emptiness; as a state of presence, fullness, overflowing and abundance; as a profound solitude yet also a profound sense of belonging; as a sense of mutuality and connectedness with the whole of existence; as a sense of letting-go and opening; as a paradoxical state of attending to a world that arises only as we attend to it – that is brought into being as we are mindful of it; as a state that is prior to, or beyond words, *and* as an awareness that is linguistically framed or determined. These are some of the ways in which the process of attending to being alive is articulated by mystics, and to some extent, by sceptics. That there are many different methods of attending to the flux of being is exemplified in the different practices developed by communities of mystics over the centuries. It is these beliefs, ideas and practices that I explore in different ways in the following pages.

Observation I – mist and clouds

I look out on mist asleep in the valley, quilting the city except for the spires of churches, a few civic buildings and the four-square cathedral – each of these a testimony to aspiration, light-headedness and a compulsion to order. Yet as I look even these obdurate monoliths quiver in the early morning sun, shivering in silvered mist like fish sometimes glint and tremble deep in an ice-covered pond. It is as if even stone and concrete, substance heaped on substance, can only make a thing that has no weight at all. So filled are they with light and atmosphere, at this distance, that it is no surprise they seem loosely tethered to the ground like so many airships shimmering expectantly with the urge to fly. I sit here at my window watching stone birds about to take wing, as the light-winged mind seeks to shake off its dogmas and prejudices, eager to be a cloud amongst clouds.

Martin Heidegger, Thomas Merton and Meister Eckhart – God as an open field of infinite possibility

Martin Heidegger has been very influential within many fields of philosophy and theology. His ideas about being and God are striking yet paradoxical – they are simultaneously incisive and vague, precise yet seemingly difficult to follow. I'd like to consider one or two strands of his notoriously enigmatic writing in order to open our enquiry into mysticism.

Heidegger has, in many ways, an ambivalent attitude towards Christianity and institutionalised religions. In his early writings he was influenced by the German Dominican monk and mystic Meister Eckhart (c.1260-1327/8), who advocated inner transformation as a goal of the religious life, believing that human beings could achieve unity with God in this life. Eckhart emphasised the ineffable nature of God, struggling to find a vocabulary that could convey God's resistance to categorisation and conceptualisation. We find in Eckhart's writings, and in Heidegger, the use of paradoxical expressions that characterise many statements made by mystics and by those who attempt to write about mystical experiences. According to Gerda von Brockhausen:

> Mystical language stands in strong contrast to rational thought. It tries to approach the ineffable by using hints, symbols, antithesis and paradox and by feeling in the dark. [....] Thus we see the importance of silence [...] for the language of mysticism. (in Schierz 2003: 40)

Eckhart refers to the ineffability of God as, "Nothingness," "Unfathomable Ocean," a "way without a way," and "dark light". (Schierz 2003: 41) Michael E. Zimmerman (1993: 241) writes about Eckhart's use of the term, "Divine Nothingness" from Heidegger's perspective:

The Divine cannot be regarded as a super entity existing somewhere else, but instead constitutes the unconditioned openness or emptiness in which all things appear. Meister Eckhart argued that humans are at one with this openness. So lacking is any distinction between one's soul and the Divine, in fact, that one who is awakened to Divine Nothingness forgets all about 'God' and lives a life of releasement (*Gelassenheit*), moved by compassion to free things from suffering.

Zimmerman identifies connections between the thinking of Eckhart and Heidegger, and it also seems appropriate to make a link with Buddhist conceptions of the *Bodhisattva*, a being who refuses to enter a state of nirvana, or complete enlightenment and freedom from suffering, until all beings have been helped to achieve this state. Zimmerman (ibid) argues that Heidegger's "notion that human existence is the openness, clearing, or nothingness in which things can manifest themselves is deeply indebted to mysticism". Heidegger extends Eckhart's notion of God as Divine Nothingness in order to describe the nature of human being. To denote human being, Heidegger uses the term *Dasein* ("being here" or "being there"), by which he means "the place in which being occurs, the openness in which presencing transpires" – to use Zimmermen's awkward, but arresting, phrase. (ibid: 244) According to Zimmerman, Heidegger proposed

that human being is not a thing but rather a peculiar kind of nothingness: the temporal-linguistic clearing, the opening, the absencing in which things can present themselves. (ibid: 242-243)

Human being in this sense is groundless, a kind of "peculiar receptivity" for the self-manifesting of entities that present themselves to us in our state of being alive. Heidegger's emphasis on receptivity and on the openness of human being, leads him to make use of Eckhart's term *Gelassenheit*, suggesting that we need to reorient our thinking and action about being towards "letting-be" rather than striving and willing. As Caputo argues, "being is not something that human thinking can conceive or grasp [...] but something that thinking can only be 'granted'". (Caputo 1993: 282) Our role is to be awake and open to being rather than to be sleepily passive:

The work that man can do is not to will but to not-will, to prepare a clearing and opening in which being may come. This is not quietism but asceticism, the hard work of a kind of poverty of spirit. (ibid)

For Heidegger human being, *Dasein*, is a process, an unfolding of possibilities, and in the work of living we have to learn to handle the contingency of what arises, the flux of events and conditions, and the complexity of weaving a thread in the web of relationships which constitutes existence. To be acutely aware of this unfolding of possibilities, to be open to what arises and to be flexible, responsive and adaptable, are qualities we need to develop if we are to experience and cope with life in all its richness and difficulty. In doing this we need to moderate the wilfulness and self-centredness of the nucleic ego, and become attuned to the relational nature of living – this means it is often necessary to unlearn, to break habits of thought, feeling and action and to "let things be" a little more.

This brings us back to the paradoxical language of mysticism and to the strategy of knowing by unknowing or opening up to nothingness as practiced by many mystics. The "grace" of mystical experience, experiencing God as a kind of existential openness, is not something that can be willed or engineered. Accounts of mystical experiences often reveal the unbidden nature of such events, in many cases they occur when all hope is lost, or when the individual has "given up", or when circumstances seem to be against the onset of such experiences. It could be argued that at such times of "letting-be" an individual may be more open and receptive to the grace of being – whether it is in Heidegger's non-theological sense or in Thomas Merton's context of Christian belief. Certainly letting-go, or non-attachment, is a key element in Buddhist practices of awakening to the flux of existence.

Happold writes of this state of letting-go in a slightly different way:

> In the *state* of Contemplation [the mystical state] there is found a self-forgetting attention, a humble receptiveness, a still and steady gazing, an intense concentration, so that emotion, will, and thought are all fused and then lost in something which is none of them, but which embraces them all. (1970: 70)

There may be a connection here between the state of Contemplation, as described by Happold and suggested by Heidegger, and states of mindfulness and non-attachment in Buddhist practices of meditation – particularly *vipassana* and *zazen*. Thomas Merton was particularly interested in exploring the potential connections between Zen Buddhism and his own contemplative tradition as a Trappist monk. His dialogues with D.T. Suzuki, whose thinking was deeply informed by the Rinzai school of Zen, trace some of the similarities and differences between the two bodies of experience. In *Mystics and Zen Masters* (1967) and *Zen and the Birds of Appetite* (1968) Merton contrasts the dualistic, Cartesian, consciousness, with its separation of subject and object, and body and mind, with another mode of consciousness which, he argues, "starts not from the thinking and self-aware subject but from Being, ontologically seen to be beyond and prior to the subject-object division". (1968: 23) Merton goes on to suggest that:

> Underlying the subjective experience of the individual self there is an immediate experience of Being. This is totally different from an experience of self-consciousness. It is completely non-objective. It has none of the split and alienation that occurs when the subject becomes aware of itself as a quasi-object. The consciousness of Being (whether considered positively or negatively and apophatically as in Buddhism) [see below, p. 49] is an immediate experience that goes beyond reflexive awareness. It is not 'consciousness *of*' but *pure consciousness*, in which the subject as such 'disappears.' (ibid: 23-24)

Merton's description here accords with the qualities of unity and oneness that have been proposed as characteristics of mystical experience – a state of non-duality that is consistent with Bertrand Russell's contention that mystical unity "refuses to admit opposition or division anywhere". (Russell 1963: 15) Merton also describes the impact that this kind of experience has on our conception and understanding of the "self". He argues that, from his Christian perspective, "The self is not its own centre and does not orbit around itself; it is centred on God, the one centre of all, which is 'everywhere and nowhere'". (Merton 1968: 24) According to Merton mystical consciousness is grounded, not in the intellect, self-awareness and acquisitiveness, but in a profound sense of the mystery, grace and sacredness of being here. He articulates a belief, shared by many mystics, that within our subjective experience of an individual self or ego lies a deeper unfathomable ocean of being of which we are simply currents or ripples. This oceanic fluid state of being is what Merton and other Christian mystics refer to as God. Merton claims that this indeterminate flux of being cannot be analysed or negotiated using the dualistic terms of conventional thought. It is more likely that we can describe or evoke the experience of such states of being by using a more allusive, poetic language – something Merton often attempts to do in his own poetry and other writings.

Suzuki, in part of his dialogue with Merton (in Merton 1968: 108-111) analyses possible connections between Eckhart's "Divine Nothingness" and "emptiness" or *sunyata* in Buddhism. [see p. 110] He relates the "metaphysical concept of emptiness" to poverty, as in the Christian sense of "blessed are those who are poor in spirit". (ibid: 108-109) He quotes Eckhart: "He is a poor man who wants nothing, knows nothing, and has nothing". (ibid: 109) This sentence brings together the Buddhist emphasis on non-attachment, freedom from desire, and the mystical idea of encountering God by entering the Cloud of Unknowing. [see p. 52] Although Suzuki and Merton acknowledge differences in terminology and modes of description between Zen and Christianity, they agree that emptiness (*sunyata*) and "Divine Nothingness" should not be seen as one side of a binary relationship, standing in opposition to "fullness" or "Everything". Instead they have to be seen as shorthand codes for states that are beyond duality and differentiation, states of dynamic betweenness, openness and indeterminacy.

Thomas Merton, thinking back on a busy day

> to say that, is to say a great deal
>
> by the time the summer was over
> I walked alone with a few trees &
> a few red brick houses
>
> mists of damp breathe the wind
>
> I would like to stop & stand,
> to enter silence in this age of crowds,
> to forget all cities, to climb the twisted stair
> & to be a flurry of wings in cool sky
>
> but in this darkness, in spite of the stillness,
> I am confronted by questions I cannot answer

Being as process: John Dewey

As we have seen above there appears to be a tension in Thomas Merton's thinking, between his desire to interrogate and celebrate the deeply mysterious process of being here, and his use of terms of transcendence in writing about being as a state or ground. As this is indicative of a profound divergence in the way mystics and others conceptualise and articulate their experiences I'd like to consider Merton's oscillating stance in relation to the ideas of John Dewey (1859-1952), the American pragmatist philosopher.

One of the key features of Dewey's thinking is the importance he attaches to experience and human action, and the way he conceptualises living and experiencing as process. These aspects of Dewey's ideas are discussed by Stephen C. Rockefeller (1989) in an essay tracing connections between Dewey and the Japanese philosopher Nishitani Keiji (1900-1990). I'm drawing heavily on Rockefeller's essay in the following remarks.

As Rockefeller points out Dewey employs a vocabulary of evolution and growth throughout his writings. As far as Dewey is concerned there is no goal or final destination towards which human beings are progressing. In Rockefeller's words, "Life is process. The self is process. The end of human life is not to attain some static ideal state and stop growing. The only end of living is to be found in a way of living". (ibid: 229) Rockefeller argues that Dewey is more concerned with becoming than with being. This is a reasonable claim. But for me (and probably for Dewey) becoming implies a goal, a direction, a leading towards something, and this can be seen as, paradoxically, a marginalisation of the *process of becoming* in favour of the intention or goal. For this reason I'm tending to use the terms being and living instead of becoming, while emphasising that being alive is a process, a state of change – hence my use of the phrase, "the flux of being or living".

For Dewey the universe is a relational field, a network of interacting and interdependent processes, constantly changing, constantly evolving. Human beings are agents within this field, weaving narratives and actions into the complex unfolding multi-dimensional tapestry of events. And it is crucial to Dewey's thinking that things *are* events. There are no "unchanging entities in the universe", as Rockefeller puts it, and there are "no unchanging Platonic essences or Aristotelian final causes and there are no immutable substances underlying the process-

es of change". (ibid: 220) Dewey argues against the idea of an absolute and eternal transcendent order. His evolutionary ideas are applied
equally to the bio-chemical sphere and to the sphere of human thought
and aspiration. For him there can be no absolute truths and eternally
valid beliefs, laws or theories. All of these are subject to evolutionary
change, open to endless revision and reformulation in the light of the
ever-changing experiences of living.

Dewey tends to be sceptical of any ideas of pure consciousness or of
consciousness somehow detached from the world in which it arises.
For Dewey there is no possibility of objective neutrality or standing
outside the flux of living in order to get a true picture of how things
are. Consciousness arises, or at least moments of consciousness are
fired by, whatever we encounter, assimilate and handle. Consciousness is a participatory activity – a manifestation of our changing relationship with whatever surrounds us and passes through us. Consciousness is a process, a doing – even when we are sitting in silent
contemplation or meditation. Even in apparent stillness there is perpetual change, the embodied mind is constantly processing the stream
of sensations and experiences.

For Dewey each entity and each stream of consciousness is unique,
acting within the relational field in a distinctive and unrepeatable way.
On the other hand each entity only exists as a thread in the web of
relationships which constitute the universe. As Rockefeller argues,
"There is real singularity and individuality in nature, but nothing exists as an isolated entity". (ibid: 221) This is as true of the human self
as it is of a lemon, a cloud or an amoeba. Diversity is integral to Dewey's conception of the universe as an "infinite complex of interacting
events". (ibid: 220) Dewey speaks of the "miscellaneous and uncoor-
dinated plurals of our actual world" (ibid: 221) – a world of ceaseless motion and interaction, about which we can never reach any conclusions, final answers or definitive theories. All we can do is try to
find an effective way of living with this unending mutability. It could
be argued that this is what Thomas Merton and other mystics and
sceptics try to do in their different ways. There is also a connection
with the process and relational ideas of Buddhism, as we shall see
below. [p. 112]

Mysticism: "this unravelling inkling"

The American poet, Amy Clampitt, in a poem entitled, Man Feeding Pigeons, while not directly saying anything about mysticism, can be interpreted as offering an unintentional and very provisional definition of mystical states of mind:

> [...] this unravelling inkling
> of the envisioned, of states of being
>
> past alteration, of all that we've
> never quite imagined except by way of
> the body: the winged proclamations,
> the wheelings, the stairways, the
> vast, concentric, paradisal rose.
> (Clampitt 1998: 299)

Note Clampitt's recognition of the body as a (or *the*) vehicle of imagination and the very provisional tentativeness of utterance, almost a whisper: "this unravelling inkling / of the envisioned". The vibrant uncertainty and round-aboutness is typical of Clampitt's poetic language. The ecstatic tone and the image of the "paradisal rose" bring to mind the mystical writings of Sufism. [see p. 62 below]

Jacob Boehme – the *Signatura Rerum* and being open to God

Jacob Boehme was a German protestant (Lutheran) theologian. Born in 1575, Boehme was trained as a shoemaker, becoming a master of his craft in 1599, eventually selling his business and giving up shoe-making in 1613. Boehme died in 1624, by which time he had written an enormous amount and gathered a following throughout Europe. Boehme was particularly interested in how to resolve the apparent incompatibility between God's infinitude and the finite actuality of human existence and understanding.

Boehme writes often about the difficulties encountered in becoming open to being in the fullest sense – that is, in his terms, being open to God. For Boehme the exercise of will, in so far as it arises from the nucleic, ego-centred self, is a hindrance to such an opening. He writes:

> Thy own hearing, willing, and seeing prevents thee from seeing and hearing God. By the exercise of your own will you separate yourself from the will of God, and by the exercise of your own seeing you see only within your own desires, while your desiring obstructs your sense of hearing by closing your ears with that which belongs to terrestrial and material things. [...] But if you keep quiet, and desist from thinking and feeling with your own personal selfhood, then will the eternal hearing, seeing, and speaking become revealed to you, and God will see and hear and perceive through you. (from Boehme's, *Supersensual Life*, 1–5, in Hartmann 1891: 41)

According to Boehme God is everywhere and in all things. Andrew Weeks explores the implications of this belief in his book, Boehme (1991). For Boehme, "God is an all-powerful, all-knowing, all-seeing, all-hearing, all-smelling, all-tasting, all-feeling God, who is everywhere". (in Weeks 1991: 56) God is both infinite in extent and yet fully present in "the smallest circumference of reality" – as Weeks puts it. (ibid: 62) This paradoxical idea of the infinite in the finite and vice versa, anticipates Baruch Spinoza's notion that the Many is contained in the One and the One in the Many. [see p. 58] For both Boehme and Spinoza this means that God and nature (the universe) are inseparable, or as Boehme suggests: "the true heavens are everywhere, even where you stand and walk". (ibid: 59)

God is manifested in every leaf, every stone and every cloud, and in every creature that exists. Human beings are just one of the manifestations of God's infinite being. In the *Signatura Rerum* (Signature of All Things), Boehme gives poetic expression to this idea of divine ubiquity. He uses the term *"Ungrund"*, literally meaning "Unground", to refer to the indeterminate and indefinable matrix out of which all things arise as if from an act of cosmic play. Weeks points out that Boehme also often uses the term, *"ungrundlich"*, which in Boehme's later writings means "unfathomable" or "incomprehensible". (ibid: 148) Given this divine indeterminacy, out of which all things arise or are manifested, it is no wonder that Boehme advises that we should be quiet and desist from over-exercising our individual will, for this is to go against the indeterminate nature of God.

One consequence of Boehme's belief in nature or "Creation" as the "Self-Revelation" of God (ibid: 189) is that he considers the universe to be a harmonious, indivisible whole, which he likens to a choir or an organ:

> The Creation is the same playing out of the Eternal Spirit upon which He plays, and is exactly like a great harmony [...] just as an organ of many voices is driven by a single wind. (ibid)

Boehme can be seen as anticipating the idea that diversity is a crucial characteristic of nature and that the diversity of all things somehow represents, in Weeks' opinion, "the plenitude and plurality of a divine will". (ibid) Though, it would seem, we need to keep in mind that this "divine will", as *Ungrund*, is indeterminate, playful – a "playing out of the Eternal Spirit". The world as a playful manifestation of divine ubiquity is a fluid and dynamic realm of exquisitely balanced and interdependent entities. In this divine order, grounded in a playful indeterminacy, freedom and multiplicity co-exist – in Boehme's view – with a hierarchical organisation of forms. This organisation or pattern is evident in all things as the "*Signatura*", the revelation of divinity as manifested in all things.

Weeks points out that this unfolding of divine being *in* the being of all things, implies that we do not have to search elsewhere or outside for a supernatural design or meaning – indeed, in a fundamental sense the "world means just what it is". (ibid: 192) For Boehme, to let go of striving, to release our attachment to what might seem to be our personal acts of will and intention, is to allow the *Ungrund* to do its work, or to play out its divine music, within us. The mystic, in Boehme's enacting of this role, is one who lets go of what we might call the egocentric or anthropocentric will in order to realise, or return to, the equilibrium and harmony of the self-revealing divinity, which is itself a manifesting of the Unground.

The dangers arising from the disequilibrium brought about by an excessive exercising of human will and its resulting actions, may strike a chord with anyone who considers the current state of environmental affairs from an ecological perspective. Certainly Boehme can be interpreted as having important things to say about the relationship between the realms of human action and the natural world. Later we'll see how a similar strategy is adopted by Daoist practitioners [p. 141] and a similar idea is put forward by Heidegger. [see his idea of *Gelassenheit*, p. 27]

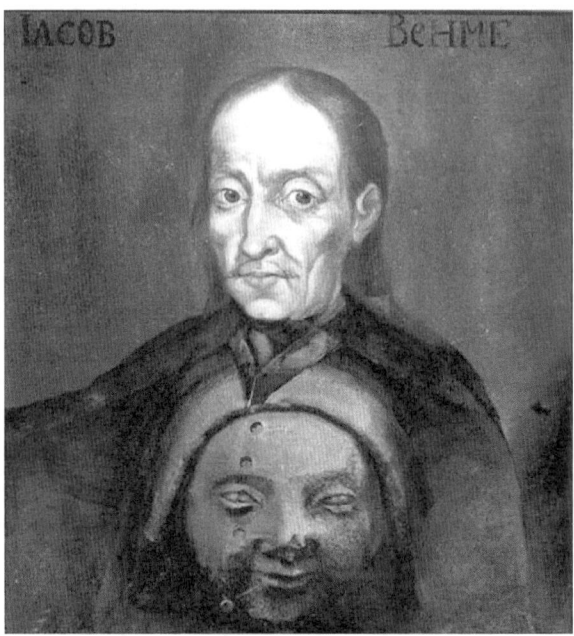

Observation II – between table and stone

On the table before me there's a drying oak-leaf and a multi-facetted, knife-sharp flint from a Dorset hill. At the leaf's edge there is a state of uncertainty, a nimbus that is neither leaf nor table, neither oak nor air, yet it is here, as integral to perception as to chemistry and metaphysics. Likewise with the flint, at its edge there is a pulse of indefinite radiance, a sensuous unknowable region which is neither stone nor table-top, neither geological punctuation nor precise position in space. It is as if both of these moments of objecthood, states of fact and self-evident truth, are also fugitives from definiteness and locality. They are not what they seem to be, while being entirely what they are: simple things within my gaze, yet also complex whisperings always out of reach of eye and comprehension – oak-leaf and stone hinting at finality yet haunted by infinitude, clouds masquerading as monoliths.

Contemplative prayer – "listening in silence"

We have seen how Thomas Merton makes some interesting com-
parisons between the practice of contemplative prayer in his own Cistercian tradition and the practice of meditation in Zen Buddhism (see
Merton 1967, 1968 & 1973) Merton suggests that in Zen meditation
(*zazen*) and in Christian contemplation, the "distinguishing, judging,
categorizing and classifying" modes of consciousness are dissolved or
let go of. (1968: 7) He goes on to suggest that what is experienced
when these modes are given up is "a *ground of openness* [...] a kind of
ontological openness", and this openness is a "radical gift". (ibid: 25)

In articulating these ideas Merton is drawing upon his readings of
Meister Eckhart, who argues that in order to realise and experience the
ground of openness, a person has to give up the conventional self –
"our special, separate cultural and religious identity", as Merton puts
it. (ibid: 12) This act of letting go is, in a very profound sense, what is
meant by poverty of spirit in the Christian mystical tradition. We have
seen how indebted Merton is to some of the ideas and terminology of
Martin Heidegger – particularly Heidegger's use of the term, *Gelassenheit*, "letting be", which Heidegger borrowed from Eckhart. Merton argues that these ideas of Eckhart's, allied to Eckhart's penchant
for paradoxical statements and images, and his use of unconventional
expressions, are all designed to "awaken his hearers to a new dimension of experience" (ibid) – which can be likened to the way in which
the paradoxical language of *koans* and anecdotes is used by Zen
teachers to awaken students to Buddha-nature or Buddha-mind. [see
below p. 127]

Merton also makes a link between what he sees as a key aspect of Zen
meditation and contemplative prayer:

> Buddhist meditation, [...] above all that of Zen, seeks not to *explain* but to *pay at-
> tention*, to *become aware*, to be *mindful*, in other words to develop a certain *kind
> of consciousness that is above and beyond deception* by verbal formulas". (ibid:
> 38)

He goes on to quote D.T. Suzuki: "Zen teaches nothing; it merely
enables us to wake up and become aware. It does not teach, it points".
(ibid: 49-50) Elsewhere Merton writes in very similar language about

Christian contemplation as being "essentially a listening in silence".
(Merton 1973: 112) And this silence is the silence of the desert, the
silence of emptiness – an emptiness full of "purity, freedom and in-
determinateness of love". (ibid: 119)

In an interesting recent book, a group of Christian contemplatives
(Cistercian, Quaker and Orthodox) use language similar to Merton's
as they discuss contemplation. Father George Timko, an American
Orthodox Christian priest, refers to the emphasis in his tradition on
contemplation as *theoria*, which he describes as "watching, observing,
simply looking. It is an interior looking of the mind, paying attention
without any expectations." (in Walker 1987: 215) John Yungblut, a
Quaker, describes this state of mind as, "waiting upon the Lord in
silence". (ibid: 202) Timko introduces the Greek term, *prosevkomai*,
which means "to move into a condition or state of being in which
there is no thought, no imaging, no desiring. It means to simply be still
and silent and quiet in a mindful state of awareness. In such a state the
(conventional, ego-based) self is dissolved". (ibid: 216)

Thomas Keating, a Cistercian monk, develops these ideas in an interesting way that again has echoes of Zen and other Buddhist practices.
It is worth quoting Keating at length:

> The habit of letting-go of thoughts and feelings, which we cultivate in contempla-
> tive prayer, is applicable to the whole of life. Before reacting to an irritating noise,
> or to an interior movement of anger or impatience, you let go of it by paying close
> attention to what is going on in the present moment. This doesn't mean [...] that
> you always renounce your own preferences. It means that your first response is to
> let go. Then you are free to decide what action to take in the light of circumstanc-
> es. The point of this practice is to forestall the compulsive habits of our emotional
> programming. (ibid: 285)

This could have been written by a Buddhist meditation teacher or by
an ancient Greek sceptic – who might use the phrase, "suspension of
judgement or belief", *epoché*, to denote the act of letting go. Keating's
comments combine practical good sense and contemplative insight –
two qualities that characterise the writings of many mystics and sceptics.

In Buddhist meditation and some forms of Christian contemplative
prayer, there is a similar emphasis on a disinterested, un-grasping ob-

servance of the embodied mind – a letting-go of the flood of thoughts, sensations, images, irritations, hopes and fears, that arise whenever we watch and listen to our unfolding consciousness. This is a strategy that Christian mystics like Eckhart and others advocate as a way of opening up to God – the open field of infinite possibility or the ground of openness.

T.S. Eliot, poetry and prayer

In his book, *T.S. Eliot and Mysticism: The Secret History of the Four Quartets*, Paul Murray puts forward some interesting ideas about Eliot's work and about the relationships between mysticism, prayer, insight and the practice of poetry. I'd like to consider various strands of Murray's argument and to relate these to aspects of scepticism.

Murray (1991: 5) suggests that Eliot considered mysticism as "a path of negation", "an ecstasy of thought" and "as an incommunicable vision". Given that Eliot seems to have attempted many times to communicate his own vision in poetry of measured intensity and lucid ambiguity, we have to recognise that paradox and contradiction are integral aspects of his method and of his aspirations. The phrase "ecstasy of thought" comes from Eliot's poem, A Song for Simeon, 1928, and Murray argues that Eliot favoured the idea of mystical ecstasy as a quality of thought rather than an effusion of feeling. In this respect, Murray contends, Eliot is closer to the views held by the Victorines of the twelfth century or by Aquinas in the thirteenth, than to the emotionalism of St. Teresa of Avila, St. John of the Cross and John Donne in the sixteenth and seventeenth centuries. Murray points out that the latter three figures were described by Eliot in 1926 as "voluptuaries of religion". (ibid: 5-6)

For Eliot religious experience, prayer and poetry are closely interwoven. Eliot's view seems to echo that expressed by Mallarmé :

> Poetry is the expression, by means of human language brought back to its essential rhythm, of the mysterious sense of existence: thus it endows our stay on earth with authenticity and constitutes the only spiritual task. (quoted by Murray 1991: 19)

Eliot strives to construct a form of poetry that is "so transparent that in reading / it we are intent on what the poetry points / at, and not on the poetry, this seems to me / the thing to try for". (ibid: 17) Of course, there is a paradox here, in that while Eliot may strive for transparency, his mode of construction, full of inter-textual references, appropriations, quotations and associations, draws attention to itself – constantly challenging the reader to question, reflect and consider divergent sources and meanings. In some ways it is this contradiction between the attempt to write poetry which points to the ineffable and the practice of poetry that draws attention to the act of pointing, which gives Eliot's work its dynamism and impact. For Eliot the practice of poetry, the making of a poem, is, like the practice of prayer, a transformative process. Eliot writes:

> Poetic originality is largely an original way of assembling the most disparate and unlikely material to make a new whole. [...] We do not imitate, we are changed; and our work is the work of the changed man; we have not borrowed, we have been quickened, and we become the bearer of a tradition. (ibid: 11)

Once again there is a paradox here: Eliot, the somewhat iconoclastic exponent of a *difficult* form of modernist poetry, considers himself as "the bearer of a tradition". Just as the mystic in writing about mystical experience does so by taking words and phrases drawn from ordinary speech, orthodox theological discourse and prayer, and re-assembling these in ways which may seem to stretch conventional syntax to breaking point, so the poet practices a similar form of appropriation, dis-integration and re-integration. The process of gathering together material from disparate sources, subjecting this material to critical questioning and dissection, and then making something out of the dissected remains, is, for Eliot, a process akin to that which occurs during prayer and contemplation. Eliot seems to have recognised a similar dialectic happening within his poetic practice and in his practice of prayer. Murray, writing about the Burnt Norton section of Four Quartets, describes this process with precision:

> [...] what I hope I have demonstrated [...] is that the dialectical process of statement and counter-statement in the poem, the discovery together for example of intense intellectual concentration with more than usual emotional distraction, the placing side by side of the abstract and the concrete, of the dogmatic and the exploratory, and the continual lively attempt to subordinate one faculty to the other – finds a most illuminating and close parallel not only in the art of music but also in the traditional practice and art of meditation and meditative poetry. (ibid: 53)

There is in Eliot's poetry a constant exploratory dynamic, a sense of seeking for what always resists being found, a restless process of enquiry that is reminiscent of the practices of many sceptics and mystics. Eliot is quite explicit about this investigatory impulse that energises his work. In the last stanza of Four Quartets he begins with the well-known lines:

We shall not cease from exploration
And the end of all our exploring
Will be to arrive where we started
And know the place for the first time.
(Eliot 1959: 59)

For Eliot, as much as for Pyrrho or Sextus,[see Part III, p. 93] what matters is the constant balancing of positive and negative, yes and no, this and that. Any assertion or idea needs to be counter-balanced by its inversion, contradiction or negation. For no human utterance constitutes the truth or the terminus of enquiry – there is always more to discover and each discovery, however small, revises the body of knowledge and opens up further possibilities and lines of enquiry. Keeping open the path of exploration is what matters. Eliot may be a Christian poet but he constantly interrogates his own experience and is wary of falling into the habit of being certain. As Murray suggests, "the immediate subject of [Eliot's] poetry is not Christian dogma, not God, but *man* in search of God". (Murray 1991: 228)

Eliot's poetry of exploration and enquiry is also a poetry of waiting, attending, being receptive to the grace of existence (which may also be the grace of God). Eliot expresses this quality of resigned waiting on what might arise in his distinctive paradoxical language. He urges us to wait:

without thought, for you are not ready for thought
[to] wait without hope
For hope would be hope for the wrong thing
[to wait even] without love
For love would be love of the wrong thing.
(ibid: 94-95)

Elsewhere Eliot, the mystical poet or poetic mystic, mutters to himself: "I said to my soul, be still, and let the dark come upon you / Which shall be the darkness of God" (ibid: 73).

Poetry, listening, praying

The Scottish poet Kathleen Jamie suggests that poets are listeners, carefully attending to the goings-on in the world, including the world of the mind:

> When we were young, we were told that poetry is about voice [...] but the older I get I think [...] it's about listening and the art of listening, listening with attention. I don't just mean with the ear; bringing the quality of attention to the world. The writers I like best are those who attend. (in Scott 2005: 23)

Jamie connects the act of attending, of listening, to the act of praying. When her husband was seriously ill with pneumonia, a friend asked if she had prayed, to which she replied that she hadn't in any formal sense. But, she went on,

> I had noticed [...] the cobwebs and the shoaling light and the way the doctor lis-
> tened and the flecked tweed of her skirt... Isn't that a kind of prayer? The care and
> maintenance of the web of our noticing, the paying heed? (ibid)

The poet, Mary Oliver, echoes Jamie's thinking in a slightly more quizzical fashion, when she writes in her poem, The Summer Day: "I don't know exactly what a prayer is. / I do know how to pay attention". (Oliver 2004: 54)

Jamie's linking of attention and prayer brings to mind a poem titled, A Journal of the Year of the Ox, by the American poet, Charles Wright, which includes a quote from *The Cloud of Unknowing*, [see p. 52] whose unknown author notes that "attention is the natural prayer of the soul". (in Spiegelman 2005: 90) Though I can't find this statement in my copy of The Cloud – indeed it is more usually ascribed to the fifteenth century French philosopher and theologian, Nicolas Male-branche – it is interesting that a poet like Wright, whose work is so concerned with a precise recording of the whole process of perception and representation, should relate this process to the act of praying.

An additional perspective on the relationship between praying and perceiving is offered by another American poet, Anthony Hecht, who suggests that the act of perceiving, particularly seeing, can provide a mode of salvation for even those poets who have never earned a living and are "no better than a viral parasite" – a phrase uttered by the speaker in Hecht's long poem, The Venetian Vespers. (Hecht 1998: 247) Hecht's poetic alter-ego suggests that the poet earns his or her keep "simply by looking". (ibid) The poet justifies his role within society by attending to phenomena and representing the act of attention in as precise and evocative a manner as possible. Interestingly, Hecht seems to practice a sceptical discipline in his poetry. The world of visual sensations is subjected to acute interrogation. Hecht turns a commonplace assumption on its head when he writes elsewhere in the same poem, "seeing is misbelieving". (ibid: 240) We have to question our perceptions if we are not to be deluded – for instance, in believing that the reeds in the lake before us all have stems bent where they meet the water's surface, or as Hecht puts it: "Seeing is misbelieving, as may be seen / By the angled stems, like fractured tibias, / Misplaced by water's anamorphosis". (ibid)

In a poem titled, Conversion of Brother Lawrence, the American poet, Denise Levertov, again echoes Jamie's thoughts about attending and praying. Levertov writes about Brother Lawrence, a seventeenth century Carmelite monk, entering "the unending 'silent secret conversation,' / the life of steadfast attention". (Levertov 1997: 46) This attention to the quotidian, the everyday, is also attention to God, to all that is, and Levertov argues that it transforms Brother Lawrence's work, infusing "even drudgery [...] with streams of sparkling color". (ibid) In the "clatter and heat of a monastery kitchen", Lawrence practices the discipline of mindfulness, attending in silent observance to the particulars of his chore-filled life, and discovers in this practice that he has opened, become more porous and receptive to the beauty and richness of being (which in Lawrence's and Levertov's terms is expressed as "God". Levertov continues: "Joyful, absorbed, / you 'practiced the presence of God' as a musician / practices hour after hour his art". (ibid: 47) Brother Lawrence's joyful state seems to be reminiscent of the state of mind of Lady Julian of Norwich (late fourteenth century) which, in another of Levertov's poems, quoting Julian, she refers to as, "*the oneing, [...] the oneing with the Godhead*". (ibid: 76)

Attending to what is here – Charles Tomlinson

The contemporary English poet, Charles Tomlinson, writes about attending to the here and now – about developing perceptual acuity as a poetic discipline. Constructing precise linguistic equivalents for articulating what it is like to be in a place, however humdrum and domestic, is an important part of Tomlinson's contemplative enquiry as a poet. In the poem, Against Travel, he writes, "These days are best when one goes nowhere, / The house a reservoir of quiet change". (Tomlinson 1997: 202) For Tomlinson it is, or it would be, more than enough if we were able to open up to the full spectrum of the phenomenal field in which we find ourselves at any moment. If we could perceive "only half" of the world that is immediately around and within us we would have no need to imagine another transcendent universe and we would have no need to believe in a transcendent being whose intentions determined the shape and direction of the world in which we stand. This world would be more than enough without resorting to speculations about another world, somehow greater, more wondrous or heavenly than this – for what could be more splendid or more real than this reality in which we participate from moment to moment? Tomlinson articulates this belief with precision and concision in his poem, Song. Here are the first three stanzas:

> To enter the real
> how far
> must we feel beyond
> the world in which we already are?
>
> It is all here
> but we are not. If we could see
> and hear only half
> the flawed symphony,
>
> we might cease
> nervously to infer
> the intentions of
> an unimaginable author
> (ibid: 195)

A key phrase is in the second stanza: "It is all here / *but we are not.*" It is as if we are absent or somehow removed from the very place in which we stand – as if we were blindfolded or shut off from our surroundings. If we could remove the blindfold, we would be able to "stand, / senses and tongues unbound". (ibid) For the poet, not to be able to perceive the full spectrum of sensory possibility is not to be able to voice that fullness – for when the senses are bound, so is the tongue. We cannot articulate in language what we are not able to experience and bring to mind. To be here, fully present to the relational universe in which we move, think and feel is the challenge that we all face if we are to realise the full potential of our lives. It is a challenge addressed with great tenacity and discipline by many of the mystics we are considering in these pages.

Nameless, limitless and beyond distinction

In Part III below, I discuss the ancient Greek sceptical belief that the suspension of judgement or belief, *epoché*, can lead to a state of inner freedom from the domination of linguistic categories (*aphasia*). The sceptics consider words as having the power to seduce and to lead, to draw us into misguided beliefs, arguments and actions – partly because verbal languages have a tendency to model the world in terms of *things*, leading us to believe that the indivisible fluidity of the cosmos is actually divided into separate entities. This sceptical attitude to verbal language has parallels with similar attitudes displayed by some Christian mystics.

In his book, *Mystics*, (2008) William Harmless has some interesting things to say about these matters. He gives an account of Meister Eckhart's ideas about the "oneness" of God, a oneness that is not reducible to number, "Eckhart's term for this is 'indistinct'". (ibid: 117-118) Harmless reminds us that when we distinguish between things, we are saying: "This is not that". In the act of identifying and naming we separate one thing from another and number them, but Eckhart argued that "God is exempt from all number". (ibid) Harmless suggests that this not mere wordplay on Eckhart's part – it is a key concept in Eckhart's theology. According to Eckhart, "God in Godself [...] is beyond distinction". (ibid: 118) Harmless goes on to point out that Eckhart also considers God to be "Nameless" – for God, "the indistinct, the numberless, cannot be named, in 'this' or 'that' terms". (ibid)

Harmless relates these ideas of Eckhart's to those of Evagrius Ponticus, a fourth century hermit, who lived for the last years of his life in a cenobitic community in the Egyptian desert. According to Harmless, Evagrius considered God to be "utterly beyond material confines – beyond shape, beyond colour, beyond time". (ibid: 151) God is infinite, indefinable and ineffable. This is not unlike Eckhart's ideas that God and the human soul share the same "ground" – *grunt*, in Eckhart's German terminology. (ibid: 127) This common ground or grounding of God and soul is a nameless, featureless, indivisible desert or wilderness – an indeterminate field.

Evagrius is well known in Christian theology for his statement that
prayer is "the conversation of the mind with God". Harmless points
out that this form of conversation is not what we might usually think
of as being a conversation, that is, an exchange of words and opinions,
instead, "as Evagrius conceived it, [conversation with God] is to move
beyond words into wordless contemplation". (ibid: 151) This form of
contemplative prayer involves not only silence, "a movement beyond
words", but also, and perhaps more importantly, it involves a "laying
aside [of] mental representations". (ibid) This "laying aside" brings to
mind Thomas Merton's suggestion that in some forms of Christian
contemplation and in the meditation practices of Zen Buddhism, it is
important to let-go of the "distinguishing, judging, categorizing and
classifying" modes of consciousness". (Merton 1968: 7) For Evagrius,
as for Merton, this "laying aside" of conceptualising forms of discourse and representational thinking, also involves a laying aside of
the conventional ego or self. While this process or state of consciousness is often described as a state of ecstasy (from the Greek, *ekstasis*,
to "stand outside" oneself), for Evagrius, prayer is not about *ekstasis*,
or leaving oneself, but "*katastasis*, a coming to one's true state" – a
returning to the stream or open field of consciousness, the permeable
or porous self. (in Harmless 2008: 152)

These ideas of Evagrius, Eckhart and Merton about language and silent prayer, can be related to what the Zen master Dogen has to say
about such matters. While I go on to discuss Dogen in more depth in
Part IV below, I'd like to consider here a few points raised by Harmless about Dogen's ideas. In his writings about *zazen* or *shikantaza*,
sitting meditation, Dogen argues that *zazen* involves neither any intention to think, in the usual sense of discursive reasoning and discriminating between one thing or idea and another, nor any intention not to
think. Rather, in *zazen*, the meditator, "neither affirms nor denies,
accepts nor rejects, believes nor disbelieves", and in so doing becomes
open to, or realises, the "presence of things as they are". (ibid: 204) To
sit in *zazen* is to *be present*, in the deepest and fullest sense of the
words. To be present, is not to seek enlightenment or to chase after
some special state of mind, instead *it is to be enlightened*, to be the
Buddha (the enlightened one). To paraphrase Dogen: to search for
enlightenment is to postpone enlightenment; to realise enlightenment
is to be present to this moment – to wake-up to the actual, to what is.

In doing so and without intending to, we are, like the sceptic and the mystic, free from the domination of linguistic categories, including names and numbers.

Observation III – under the yew tree

The yew tree stands dark, overhanging the old shed. At the tip of each branch new bright-green flattened needles grow an inch or so, not much more, adding their season's weight to the bulk of years gone by. Lower down each branch, other needles turn pale-ochre, releasing chemicals of growth and sustenance back into the veins of the tree. As the hot days move on, the pale-ochre turns paler and each desiccated needle eventually spins and spirals to the ground. Under the tree these tiny, almost weightless, shards of yew-skin break down and become one. The crust they form is so dense very few plants can grow in the yew-dark shade.

Saying and unsaying – *apophatic* and *kataphatic* traditions

On pages 102-105 I discuss Michel de Montaigne's use of sceptical methods to strip away false certainties, beliefs and dogmas. Montaigne is equally rigorous in his interrogation of Christian orthodoxies and dogmatic assertions but he nonetheless remains a Christian. It is as if he uses a sceptical method to show to himself and to others the folly of making any kind of credible statement or judgement about the nature of God or about our relationship with God. For Montaigne, God seems to be a remainder, a possibility left over from the exercise of doubt and critical enquiry. While this unfolding of argumentation may seem surprising or even illogical it is a dialectical turn which has a history in the discourses of mystics and theologians, and can be linked to a longstanding debate centring on two seemingly oppositional terms and ideas: *apophasis* and *kataphasis* (occasionally spelt: *cataphasis*).

Mysticism is often theorised as taking two main forms: one, the *via positiva* – which contends that mystical states of consciousness (the awareness of God or the flux of being) can be sought utilising techniques and methods that develop ordinary modes of cognition (if to a heightened, more intense, degree) and which can be formulated in propositional terms in verbal language; the other form is often referred to as the *via negativa* – which contends that only a process of negation and unlearning can lead to mystical states of awareness and only a language of negation can describe or evoke such states. These two forms can also be associated with two contrasting ways in which mystics and theologians write about and describe mystical states: *apophasis* and *kataphasis* – the former commonly taken as referring to a negative discourse and the latter referring to a positive discourse.

According to Michael A. Sells, this interpretation is too simplistic and potentially misleading. He argues that we need to be more precise in interpreting these two terms, taking account of their etymology. *Apophasis* comes from the Greek, *apo phasis* meaning "un-saying or speaking-away". *Kataphasis* is another Greek term meaning "affirmation, saying, speaking-with". (Sells 1994: 2-3) Sells suggests that these two terms and the actions they denote need to be considered as having a dialectical relationship, and it is the reciprocity and alternation between "saying" and "unsaying" that gives meaning to mystical discourse. Hence we find in the writings of many, if not most, mystics a continual oscillation between affirmative statements and retractions or denials of such statements. Saying and unsaying are interwoven in a spiralling of utterance and counter-utterance, proposition and opposition, speech and silence. It is out of this dialectical tension that mystical states of consciousness are framed and given voice.

Within *kataphatic* modes of discourse, emphasis is placed on making affirmative statements, on *saying*; within *apophatic* modes, emphasis is placed on retraction, on *unsaying* – for even the most determined exponent of *apophatic* modes of mystical discourse, if they are to speak or write at all, must say in order to unsay. Mystics within the *apophatic* traditions resort not only to negating the positive propositions that characterise conventional modes of speech, but they also negate the negation. This dialectical process is reminiscent of similar ways of speaking and writing in sceptical literature – every proposition or argument can be countered with an opposing proposition or argument, a process which leads the sceptic to conclude that there is no conclusion and therefore it is reasonable and necessary to suspend

judgement. [see p. 95] There are also similarities in relation to a dialectics of affirmation and negation in both Madhyamika and Zen
schools of Buddhism. [see Part IV]

Kataphasis can also be associated with revelation, disclosure and
light; *apophasis* with hiddeness, absence and darkness. Denys Turner
takes up this thread of associations in his book, *The Darkness of God:
Negativity in Christian Mysticism.* (1998) While Turner's line of argument is very contentious and opposed by many scholars I'd like to
briefly consider his comments about saying and unsaying, absence and
presence, lightness and darkness. As if continuing Sells' line of
thought, Turner uses the term "self-subverting utterance" to denote
"the utterance which first says something and then, in the same image,
unsays it". (Turner 1998: 21) He gives as an example phrases used by
Denys the Areopagite (also known as Pseudo-Dionysius):

> The divine light is a 'brilliant darkness'; the 'mysteries of God's word' are uttered
> in a 'hidden silence'. [...] Denys [also] says that on the highest peaks of
> knowledge 'one is neither oneself nor someone else'. (ibid)

For Turner these statements of Denys are intentionally paradoxical,
constituting the "natural linguistic medium" of a language that seeks
"both to affirm and deny all things of God". (ibid: 22) Even the apparent contradiction between affirmation and denial has to be affirmed
and denied. Turner argues that *apophasis* "is the linguistic strategy of
somehow showing by means of language that which is beyond language". (ibid: 34) Echoing Sells, Turner implies that this "linguistic
strategy" is a dialectical process – a dialectics of affirmation and negation, paradox and contradiction. He reminds us that this linguistic
strategy is not a rhetorical device designed to entertain or surprise, it
has a very serious purpose. He writes: "[Meister Eckhart uses] speech,
necessarily broken, contradictory, absurd, paradoxical, conceptually
hyperbolic speech, to bring to insight the ineffability of God". (ibid:
151) This brings to mind the ways in which a language of paradox and
contradiction is used by Zen teachers to bring their students to a realisation of Buddha nature, to become aware of *that which is* as a manifestation of the whole relational field of existence. [see p. 112 below]

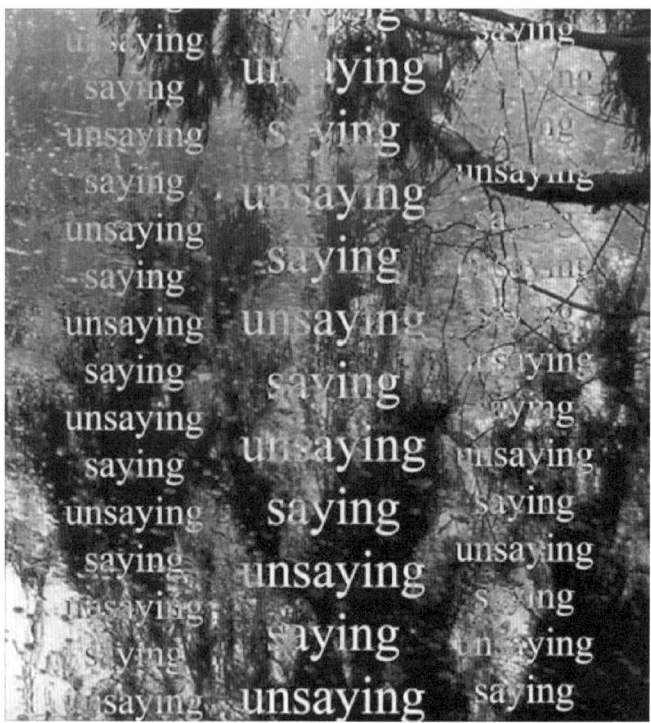

The "Cloud of Unknowing" – forgetting the self

In the writings of many mystics, from theistic and non-theistic traditions, there is an emphasis on letting-go of the self, in its conventional ego-centred form, in order to experience a very different state of being. Theists might describe this state as an experience of God or a becoming one with God – God as a boundless, undifferentiated, ineffable openness. Non-theists might refer to this state as a state of being or as a realisation of the relational nature of things, things as they are – Buddha-nature, Buddha-mind or the Dao. In all cases there is an acknowledgement that in order to realise these different states of consciousness the conventional, discriminating, ego-centred self has to be radically re-structured, re-formulated or dissolved.

The unknown author (there is evidence he was male) of the late four-teenth century Christian text, *The Cloud of Unknowing* (ed. Wolters 1961), advises his readers how to become aware of God. The language used is *apophatic* – full of paradoxes and reciprocal affirmations and negations. God is described as being in darkness, beyond or outside, rational thought and discursive language. The author argues that it is important "'to trample on' thoughts that arise (even those about God), even when they 'seem to be holy'". (ibid: 60) In order to become conscious of God we have put away thoughts "deep down in the cloud of forgetting", only then can we penetrate the "cloud of unknowing" between us and God. It is only by reducing the ceaseless chatter of the inner voice, (which is the voice of the wilful self and personal desire, *not* the voice of God), that we can open up to the presence of God. (ibid:61)

As a method for forgetting, the author advises his disciple to use "a word", the shorter the better, as a refrain, chant or prayer. This repeated word is not a thought, argument or supplication addressed to God, but a simple device with which to "suppress all thought under the cloud of forgetting". (ibid) This disciplined attention, focusing on the chosen word, is needed to enable us not to "feed" on the distractions of thoughts, which maintain and manifest the conditional self, however pure of heart or spiritual these thoughts may seem. It is only when we "forget" the self and its images, arguments, rational thoughts and desires that we can enter and pass through the "cloud of unknowing", that we can blindly grope "for the naked being of God". (ibid: 64)

The references to a "cloud of forgetting" and a "cloud of unknowing" is reminiscent of the idea of "knowing ignorance" (*docta ignorantia*, in Latin) put forward by Nicholas of Cusa (also known as Cusanus) in the fifteenth century. Cusanus, like the author of *The Cloud*, presents his ideas in the paradoxical language of the *apophatic* tradition. Cusanus writes about his first "revelation" or mystical insight, on board a ship bound for Venice from Constantinople in c.1437-1438. He claims that by a "heavenly gift from the father of light" he was able to "embrace incomprehensibles incomprehensibly in knowing ignorance, by the passing beyond incorruptible truths humanly knowable". (in Cranz 2000: 3) Cusanus, who was also a mathematician, stretches rational language to its limits in this statement. Edward Cranz argues that Cusanus considered God as the Absolute, to be beyond reason and intellect, and yet what is beyond reason can somehow touch the mind through an incomprehensible embracing of what is incomprehensible. This is the "knowing ignorance" that Cusanus believes we have to make use of if we are to engage with God.

Although Cusanus uses the language of transcendence to articulate his thoughts, the idea of "knowing ignorance" can be related to the mode of awareness employed by Buddhist practitioners when observing the flux of living while sitting in meditation. Observing the stream of phenomena that arises in the embodied mind from moment to moment, without adding a commentary or making judgements on such phenomena can be seen as a way of exercising "knowing ignorance" – trying to be aware while also letting go of thoughts, feelings and perceptions can be seen as a way of not imposing habits of thought and assumptions upon the process of being here. [see notes on Buddhism in Part IV]

The many modes of silence

There are a multitude of references to silence in mystical literature – silence equated with God, with the flux of being, with emptiness, with the stony face of a desert and with poverty of spirit. Silence can take many forms and it is to these different modes of silence that Oliver Davies turns in an essay entitled, Soundings: towards a theological poetics of silence. (in Davies & Turner 2002) Davies distinguishes between two main kinds of silence: "silence as the absence of noise and silence as the cessation of speech". (ibid: 202) He uses two Russian words to denote these very different modes. It is worth quoting his remarks at length:

> The former I shall designate by the Russian word *tishina*, [which] denotes the silence of the forest, or of the tundra, and carries with it some sense of the English word 'stillness'. The latter I shall call *molchanie*, which denotes silence maintained by someone who speaks. The former [...] is a silence which speech breaks, while the latter is a silence of speech. Thus a conversation in the Russian forest will banish silence as *tishina*, but creates the possibility of silence as *molchanie*. These two silences are constantly in tension. (ibid)

Mystical theology to some extent oscillates between studies of these two modes of silence.

Davies argues that *tishina*, the silence of the forest, within the Judaeo-Christian traditions, is identified "with God, who is eternal and infinite, and who, as silence, is the primordial and generative ground" out of which words, as divine utterance and the speech of human beings, arise. (ibid: 203) According to Turner, "the transcendent, unoriginate and infinite God who is one with silence, who is silence, chooses to break that silence by speaking". (ibid) This act can lead us to ask many questions, for instance: if God is silence, infinite, boundless and indivisible, what happens when He speaks, when he utters the divine "Word" and graces human beings and other creatures with speech, signs and gestures? Is the silence broken? If so, what has happened to God? Is God now a silence that somehow contains sound, or is God no longer infinite and boundless – a God bounded in the act of gracing creatures with speech? Once the infinite potentiality of God (God as all that is possible) is realised or actualised in any word (or being or event), is there no longer infinite potentiality – and possibly, therefore, no God? These are some of the questions and paradoxes that have been argued over for centuries by theologians and writer mystics.

One further thought arising from Davies's essay concerns the many registers of silence in its *molchanie* form – the silence that occurs when speech is suspended for a moment or for a longer period. In this instance, silence can have many meanings and roles in the course of speaking. It can be: aggressive, resigned, expectant; it can be the silence of friends or lovers who enjoy each other's company, the silence of enemies who distrust each other and cannot speak openly, the silence of anger, the silence of grief, astonishment, perplexity or embarrassment, and so on. These subsidiary forms arise once utterance becomes conversation, dialogue and debate. And these conversations grow into the hubbub of voices, languages and signs that are considered by many mystical writers (and poets) as obscuring God, the infinite silence – as if we wander along a path between tall trees, arguing about the nature of God, reality and mysticism, and in so doing we are no longer able to hear the silence of the forest. With each footfall and word we seem to destroy or postpone the realisation of our quest.

Saint Teresa: the absurdity and necessity of writing

The literature of mysticism is vast. In many traditions, across many religions, mystics have written at great length about states of consciousness that seem to be beyond description. Acres of forests continue to be felled to provide paper for books about *tishina*, the silence of the forest – the infinite silence of God, the ineffable presence of what is. There is a widespread uncertainty amongst many mystic writers about the efficacy of writing about their experiences and beliefs. Saint Teresa of Avila, (1515-1582) was a Spanish Carmelite nun, renowned for her writings about contemplative prayer. Until her late twenties she read a lot but became distrustful of written knowledge and, according to Robert Petersson, questioned the value of her nuns learning Latin or even reading the bible. (in Petersson 1970: 19) Petersson argues that Teresa was distrustful of all "knowledge not drawn from direct experience", believing "that reading could distract her and others from meditation and good acts". (ibid)

Nevertheless, Teresa goes on to write at length about her experiences and about the methods she advocates to her fellow nuns, but there is often an ambivalence in what she has to say about reading and writing. When writing about the difficulties of "standing outside oneself" she suggests that the attempt to describe or explain such a struggle "may very well be foolish". (ibid: 25) Petersson argues that no matter what means Teresa, and other mystics, use "to close the gap between the word and the thing [...] every account we read is marred by one defect or another". (ibid) Even the use of "metaphor, hyperbole, and paradox" fails to achieve more than an indirect pointing to the unsayable sublimity of the states of consciousness the mystic attempts to describe. Orthodox grammar and speech may be bent, inverted, turned inside out in what may seem in the end to be a fruitless attempt to construct a poetic transcription or evocation of contemplative states of being here.

Although Teresa writes in praise of God, her attempts, she says, constitute no more than "a thousand holy absurdities". (ibid: 31) Petersson suggests that it is only when "deeply immersed in prayer" that her consciousness becomes so transparent and porous that she displays a skill very like "the gift of tongues". (ibid) It is as if, in prayer, she acts as an agent for something outside herself to speak – as if, as Petersson puts it, "her pen were a needle copying out a pattern clearly laid down before her eyes". (ibid)

Not knowing what to say

All dried up, held to a lip and stuck.
Flow slows, seeps to a stop. Sun-skinned
mud becomes thin silver carcass of a
pewter river. Just the way words do,
dried to a haltingness, a dull stump. Not
because there is no weight of liquid to
prompt them, but to leave off as of
turning the page. The not-saying as
eloquent as the drum of speech on a
taut ear

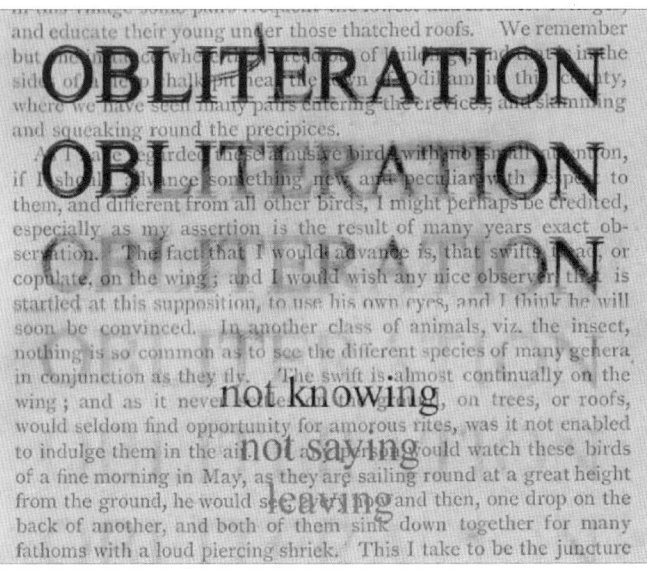

Another perspective on mysticism and God: Baruch Spinoza

Although the Dutch philosopher, Baruch Spinoza (1632-1677) was, by all accounts, a mild-mannered, honest, tolerant and prudent man, much-loved by those who knew him, even by many of those who disagreed with him, his ideas were extremely controversial. Although he was born a Jew and was obviously a religious man who wrote a lot about God, he was rejected by both the Jewish and Christian establishments – many of whose congregations considered him to be an atheist or a dangerous subversive. If he hadn't been able to live quietly in Holland making his living by polishing lenses, he would have had a difficult time living anywhere in Europe. The Dutch government was very tolerant of independent theological thinkers – something that was not true of most seventeenth century European governments. (Russell 1946: 592-603)

So what were the ideas that Spinoza was putting forward that disturbed so many of his contemporaries? In the *Ethics*, which was published just after he died in 1677, he argues for a new way of thinking about God, nature and human moral behaviour. He maintains that, "There is only one substance, 'God or Nature'; nothing finite is self-subsistent". (ibid: 594) Individual entities, objects or things are all "merely aspects of the divine Being", (ibid) whose being is infinite and therefore must include everything. It is only the infinite everything, the universe as a whole, that is "self-subsistent", the one infinite undifferentiated substance. Every *thing* can only be a part of that totality, a subsistent aspect of the whole, dependent for its existence on all the other parts of the whole. According to Quinton (in Magee 1987: 101) Spinoza is only logically developing Descartes' definition of substance as "that which requires nothing but itself in order to exist". For the deeply religious Spinoza this meant that, in Quinton's words, "the only true substance is God". Therefore for Spinoza, the infinitude of God means there can be nothing outside of God, because if there were anything outside God it would follow that God had boundaries and was therefore finite. "If God is infinite then God must be co-extensive with everything". (ibid: 102) Looked at from another perspective, if "nature is the totality of what there is," (Quinton, ibid) then both God and Nature must be infinite and therefore they must be identical, one unitary substance.

For Spinoza every *entity* exists only insofar as it is part of the totality of all of existence. This idea can be seen as articulating, in a very different cultural, historical and geographical context, similar insights to those we will encounter in relation to Madhyamika philosophy. [p. 110 below] Spinoza, like Madhyamika Buddhists, argues that it is only by conventions of thought and language that objects, ideas and things can be considered as separate or discrete, for in truth they are all interdependent aspects of an infinite and indeterminate reality – they lack self-subsistence. According to Russell (1946: 596), "Spinoza, like Socrates and Plato, [and, we might add, the Buddha] believes that all wrong action is due to intellectual error: the man who adequately understands his own circumstances will act wisely". Understanding comes through disciplined attention to how things are in the world, through practices that develop the critical powers of the mind leading to an intense clarity of awareness. This includes an acute awareness of the relative, conventionalised reality of linguistic structures, rationality and reification, and also a clear recognition of the misguided beliefs, values and behaviours that arise from treating this reality as a true or absolute state of affairs.

Our desire to own or consume what we have reified and divided into *objects*, causes us endless frustration and dissatisfaction. We are trapped in our dualistic thinking. We want to hang on to what is passing, clinging to fictional substances temporarily held apart from everything that is. This misguided habitual attachment to any part of the whole, as if it were truly separate and self-subsisting, is a failure to understand the mutuality of existence, the interdependence of everything. These misguided attachments to objects (houses, cars, money, status, roles, ideas, beliefs and values), as if they were absolutes, can be linked to what Spinoza describes as our bondage to "the passions", those reactive emotions like hatred, anger, fear and envy, "in which we appear to ourselves to be passive in the power of outside forces". (ibid: 598) Russell quotes Spinoza: "An emotion which is a passion ceases to be a passion as soon as we form a clear and distinct idea of it". (ibid) In other words, once we understand *and accept* the relative nature of reality we no longer feel an obsessive attachment to any part of it. Russell: "In so far as a man is an unwilling part of a larger whole, he is in bondage; but in so far as, through the understanding, he has grasped the sole reality of the whole, he is free". (ibid)

Another aspect of Spinoza's thinking that upset Christians and Jews alike was his view that even sins and other moral failings, in so far as they were an integral part of the whole, are only sins and failings seen from the finite perspective of human beings. As Russell puts it, "In God, who alone is completely real, there is no negation, and therefore the evil in what to us seem sins does not exist when they are viewed as parts of the whole". (ibid: 594) This does not mean that the notion of "sin" has no meaning or value within the realm of human affairs, it only points to the relative nature of sin, however conceived. Sins and moral structures are not absolutes. This relativism contributed to Spinoza's wise generosity of spirit. He advised that we should develop the "active emotions" including happiness, love and tolerance, which are grounded in understanding, rather than cultivate (or repress) the passive emotions such as anger, resentment and frustration, which are caused by conditions or circumstances outside our control. And the highest of the active emotions "is what he calls 'the intellectual love of God', the emotion that attends metaphysical understanding, a comprehensive grasp of the nature of the world as a whole". (Magee 1987: 106)

Spinoza's conceptualisation of "God" can be interpreted as offering a possible alternative to the more usual Christian idea of God as a personalised yet transcendent entity. Implicitly, if not overtly, Spinoza emphasises the importance of attending to *this* world as a manifestation of God, indeed *as God*, rather than emphasising the importance of attending to another world, a speculative utopian transcendent reality beyond this one. To be aware of being *here*, being a part of this contingent reality of relationship and mutuality, *is* to be aware of God. For Spinoza, this profound contemplation of the interdependent and interrelated nature of the universe, gives rise to an equally profound sense of wonder and respect for all aspects of reality, all manifestations of existence.

Observation IV – intermingling

Vancouver Island, 1974. I lie in bed watching galaxies of dust spinning through a shaft of sunlight that angles down into our basement crypt from the one ground-level, lawn-high window. A dusty sagging cobweb wafts in the breeze of my own deep-morning breathing. Last night I sat on the shaky wooden veranda watching the lazy late summer air begin to tighten towards autumn. All around the sound of snoring bees mingled with the delicious after-taste of a mushroom pie. Down in the sheltered garden there's a patch of swiss chard, a file of red cabbages, a few gothic brussel sprouts, beetroot, tomatoes heavy with fruit desperately trying to stay upright against the garage wall. A tiny blonde moth tumbles and turns between the blades of grass, silvery with dew. A few crumpled dandelions sit in the shadows like silent Harpo Marxs. Over the fence a crystalline rainbow arcs through a spray watering the lawn. Every now and again three kids dash into the spray, bursting the rainbow into a multitude of prisms that hang for a moment on their eyelashes and on the tips of their fingers. Just behind them a pool of sunlight warms the wet trunk of an apple tree. Now it's all gone. Here in our quiet cell I catch faint echoes of yesterday, spangled memories suspended in another time.

Thomas Merton and Sufism

To end this chapter I'm going to return to the writings of Thomas
Merton, particularly his comments on aspects of Sufism. Sufism is
often described as the mystical branch of Islam. Practitioners of Sufism believe that it is possible to become close to God, to embrace the
Divine Presence, in this life, in preparation for an even closer encounter with God after death in paradise. Merton's interest in Sufism was
longstanding and his writings include numerous references to the beliefs and practices of the Sufis. According to Seyyad Hossein Nasr,
Merton was very attracted to the Sufi view that nature is "the self-
revelation, unveiling, and theophany of God" and that "all phenomena
[are seen] as Divine Signs (*vestigial Dei*)". (in Baker & Henry 1999:
11) These beliefs are reminiscent of the beliefs of the early Christian
desert mystics who saw the universe as a manifestation of Divine
creativity. Merton writes about these ideas in his book, *The Wisdom of
the Desert*, (Merton 1970). There are also echoes here of the beliefs of
Jacob Boehme [see above, p. 33] and Meister Eckhart. [p. 26]

There are many stages on the Sufi path, these include: "search, love,
gnosis, independence, *tawhîd* [a realisation of the oneness of God] and
bewilderment [*dahash*, in Arabic]". (Thurston in Baker & Henry
1999: 34) Robert Thurston argues that bewilderment is an important
state of mind for the Sufi mystic on the path towards self-knowledge
and spiritual realisation. (ibid) This is something that echoes Merton's
own statement, quoted by Thurston: "We get into total bewilderment,
we lose our own hearts". (ibid) This state of bewilderment, uncertainty
and puzzlement is indicative of a person beginning to let go of the
conventional ego-centred self. And this is what the Sufi method involves, for the final stage on the Sufi path is *fanâ* – translated from the
Arabic as "annihilation", "extinction" or "passing away". (ibid: 36) In
order to realise Divine Unity, the self has to be extinguished, to pass
away – for if, as the Sufi believes, God is One there can be no self
separate from God. The Sufi path is a path away from all dualities,
distinctions and divisions, a return to the primordial state of unity.
Again note the echoes of Boehme, Eckhart and Spinoza. [p. 58]

Thurston describes how Merton studied the prayer methods of the
Sufis, particularly *dhikr*, which includes breath control, counting the

breaths and contemplation focused on God. According to Thurston, Merton described to his novice monks the Sufi method of learning *dhikr*. This involved a Sufi disciple sitting in front of his teacher and breathing in time with each other. Thurston writes:

> The disciple follows the master and starts saying the *shahâdah* as he exhales: "La ilâha illa 'Llâh." This becomes a total renunciation of everything except God. In this process the disciple concentrates on what is happening. He thinks: "I want nothing, I love nothing, I seek nothing but God. (ibid: 37)

The *shahâdah* involves the recitation of the words meaning there is "no god but God", the fundamental Islamic belief that there is only one God and that God is One. *Dhikr* also takes the form of reciting the Names of God. The practice of *dhikr* brings to mind the Christian practice of reciting the Jesus prayer (*kyrie eleison* or "Christ have mercy"), the Buddhist practices of breath control and counting, and the reciting of the phrase, *namu amida butsu*, in Japanese Shin Buddhism. One of the purposes of all these practices is to re-orientate consciousness away from an ego-centric position, to let go of the limited conventional self in order to realise emptiness, Divine Unity or Buddha-mind – or whichever term is used in a particular tradition of mystical writing.

Shaikh ad-Darqâwî condenses these ideas into a memorable sentence: "if you were to examine yourself, you would find God instead of finding yourself, and there would be nothing left of you but a name without a form". (my version of a quote in Baker & Henry 1999: 172) This is uncannily similar to Dogen's famous statement:

> To study the Way is to study the self.
> To study the self is to forget the self.
> To forget the self is to be enlightened by all things.
> To be enlightened by all things is to remove the barriers between one's self and others. (Dogen 2009)

Silhouette: Thomas Traherne

I was a stranger   from dust I rose   in my bones
was knowledge   all things were spotless & pure &
nothing in the world   and yet out of nothing all
tears & quarrels were brought to pass   in silence
did I see how soft the stars did entertain my senses
these eyes & hands did seek the lofty skies & touch
chaos   all that is born dies into the dust of light
from which all things rise: trees & wheat, lively air &
time, smiles & sorrows, rare & ordinary things

[Composed from fragments of texts used by Gerald Finzi
in *Dies Natalis*, opus 8 – including quotes from Traherne's
Centuries of Meditation and from Arioso]

from dust

all tears and quarrels

rise into the light

and become light

nothing prior to the word

words   words

    no primary substance

    words words words words

    words words words words

    words talk words words

    words words talk words

    words words words words

no foundation

so much to say

          so
        much
     chatter

talk talk talk

no reality unmediated by language

Part II

Mysticism, language and postmodernism

> "Emotions or passions may be set going
> by words attached to events rather than
> directly by events themselves
> – by *nomos* or convention [...]
> rather than by *physis* or nature".
> (McEvilley 2002: 421)
>
> "Open your mouth, you are lost,
> close your mouth, you are lost".
> (Wright 2001: 53)

Introduction

A few of the key figures within postmodern literature and philosophy have explored aspects of mystical thought and identified connections between their own ideas and practices and those of mystic writers in the east and west – I'm thinking particularly of Jacques Derrida and Roland Barthes. Other authors have drawn parallels between aspects of the literature of mysticism and the discourses of postmodernism – for instance: John D. Caputo, Michael E. Zimmerman, Denys Turner, Don Cupitt and Michael A. Sells. These investigations, into the apparent affinities between mysticism and postmodernism, are particularly focused on language/discourse, deconstruction and dialectical method. In the background of many of these interesting and challenging dialogues lies the work of Heidegger, who has undoubtedly prompted many of the lines of enquiry pursued by the above writers. In this chapter I'm going to consider some of the ideas and issues raised by this conversation between two apparently very different fields of thought and practice.

Don Cupitt – "a mysticism of secondariness"

In his book, *Mysticism after modernity*, (1998) Don Cupitt provides a typically challenging postmodern view of the literature of mysticism – and we ought to note that for Cupitt mysticism *is primarily* a mode of linguistic discourse, a matter of words, signs and the particular religious contexts out of which the literature arises. I'd like to consider some of Cupitt's ideas at length as they can be seen as representing the position taken by many contemporary postmodern writers, who are themselves heirs of structuralism, post-structuralism and semiology in its many forms – fields of study that all take as given a focus on language and on deconstruction as an important analytical tool.

Cupitt argues against any idea that mysticism, and religion, have anything to do with accessing any other world than this one. He is very critical of the "older 'platonic' kind of mysticism" which involved "a special supernatural way of knowing something Higher that was itself [...] super-natural". This "older kind of mysticism" was a manifestation of a body of religious thought "associated with philosophical rationalism and a two-worlds cosmology". (Cupitt 1998: 7) In place of this older version of mysticism, Cupitt argues for a "mysticism of secondariness", that is a mysticism in which, "there is no specially privileged and secure starting-point, first principle or foundation from which to start". (ibid: 7) As far as Cupitt is concerned there is no transcendent other, or absolute reality, or ground of being:

> There is no pure datum, no primary substance, no "absolute", nothing that is always ontologically prior. Nothing is always real from every point of view. We are always in secondariness. (ibid)

Though Cupitt points out that, "language may not give us a rock-solid starting point. It too is secondary", he does have a tendency to give language a special kind of status. Indeed, later in the book he makes an eloquent argument for language as a kind of "primary substance". (ibid: 74) He is arguing against the "Modern view of mysticism" in which:

> [...] the mystics first had great and ineffable experiences, in states of consciousness that were prior to and outside language, and then they subsequently tried to put into inadequate words what they had experienced". (ibid)

He goes on:

> I reject that theory. There is no such thing as "experience", outside of and prior to language. The Modern idea of the mind as an inner theatre, and of experience as a show seen by an audience of one, is itself a secondary cultural and literary creation. It doesn't exist! *Language goes all the way down.* [my italics] Language doesn't copy or convey experience; language determines or forms experience as such. [...] Language *is* mind: I mean, what we call the "the mind" is secondary; it is an effect of language. (ibid)

Note the dogmatic certitude with which Cupitt makes his case. There is no doubt *in his mind* that mind "is an effect of language" or that "language goes all the way down" – which sounds very close to asserting that language *is* primary. In this passage, which expresses a basic tenet of his thesis regarding mysticism, Cupitt articulates the orthodox postmodern position that there can be nothing outside or before language. From Saussure onwards this has been the essential dogma of the anti-essentialist postmoderns, voiced in different ways by Derrida, Baudrillard, Irigaray, Kristeva, and by most semiologists and semioticians, structuralists and poststructuralists. The linguistic turn in philosophy is predicated on the belief that, at the very least, human experience is always mediated through language, or, in its more extreme form, that language *is* experience, or is reality – everything is a manifestation of language, everything is a linguistic construction.

This rhetoric of "secondariness" is very seductive, particularly for thinkers whose primary mode of working is talking and writing. But it may be useful to maintain at least some degree of scepticism about these claims. Is the mind "an effect of language"? If I sit in the garden, quietly watching the movement of trees, leaves, birds and passing planes – seeing, hearing, tasting the air, feeling the pulse of blood through my body and the moods and emotions that come and go. If I sit in this way and don't verbalise these experiences until now, when I write them down, am I to say that, *at the time they occurred*, I was mindless – or was I perhaps, mindful? If I imagine a sequence of images, remember places I've been to, faces I've seen, or imagine things I haven't yet seen, if I do these things wordlessly, silently, are these non-linguistic experiences somehow not experiences at all, or not manifestations of mind? Can there be no silent, non-linguistic experiences?

Cupitt exaggerates his case, and appears to close his mind to many kinds of mental operations and experiences that are not linguistic. Is this because he finds it impossible to stop the ceaseless chattering of his own internal voices, or does he tend to ignore or devalue the silent times? As the practice of mindfulness, prayer and meditation can demonstrate, there can be silent attention without verbal commentary, it is possible to be conscious and not to be linguistically active – silent, wordless being can be a time of mental acuity, vividness of perception and intensity of experience, some of which we might even refer to as mystical.

Cupitt asks, rhetorically, "how can there be *knowledge* that is prior to language?" (ibid: 34) He implies that there can't. But this seems a quirky dogma to espouse. Does he mean that all knowledge is *de facto* expressible in words? In which case of course, there can be no knowledge that is not demonstrable through verbal language. But if we recognise a broader idea of what constitutes knowledge (for instance, including to *know how* to do something or to identify something) then it is reasonable to question Cupitt's assertion. Does he believe that one can't know how to ride a horse or a bicycle, hum a tune or breath, without having language, that is, verbal language (for Cupitt seems, more often than not, to be talking about verbal language – he is curiously reticent about visual symbolic orders or languages) or without being able to formulate such knowledge in a linguistic construct. Surely being *shown* how to do something (in silence) is not only a valid way of learning or coming-to-know, it may even be the most effective way (for instance, in relation to playing a piano, drawing a horse, building a wall or writing the letter A).

Elsewhere Cupitt asks, again rhetorically, "how can one describe a state as being indescribable?" (ibid: 33) An assertion that, he suggests, is self-defeating – which it is if one holds tightly to the idea that there is nothing prior to, or beyond, verbal language. But it could be that in making such a statement we are simply acknowledging that verbal language has limits, while also pointing to something (a feeling, emotion, state of mind, visual image or sensation) that is outside the linguistic realm. It may be that the job of describing can be done better through the act of showing without necessarily using words (for instance, in drawings, paintings, sculpture, music or dance). It could also be that the contortions of a poet bending, subverting or contravening the rules of propositional discourse or rational argument – through the use of paradox, contradiction, negation, allusion and absurdity – may be doing so precisely because she is trying to point to something outside of language. This *something* might be the felt actuality of a sensation, or a sense of the otherness of nature, the cosmos or even what we might call God.

A sceptic might argue that we should place all positions, points of view, assertions and beliefs, in brackets – questioning them all in equal measure, seeing them all as limited, provisional, open to argument, contradiction and refutation. To be sceptical about only one side of an argument is a form of dogmatism. In relation to Cupitt's argument it may be useful to suggest that it *is possible* that there is something, or a state of affairs, prior to, or outside, language, *and* that there isn't, *and* that there neither is nor isn't. We don't know for sure, but it may be more useful and more interesting to be open to all possibilities as we move on from question to question, uncertainty to uncertainty. And *not knowing*, suspending belief, is a key aspect of sceptical dialectics. But Cupitt doesn't seem to like uncertainty, any more than the supernaturalists or modernists he argues against. Montaigne suggests that we might keep in mind an image of a set of scales or seesaw, hovering at a point of balance between one possibility and another, between each proposition and its opposite. This would seem to be a wise and useful course of action.

Paradoxically, Cupitt seems to acknowledge the potential importance of unknowing, silence and doubt, even if in much of his writing he adopts a rather dogmatic tone and seems ill-at-ease with uncertainty or ineffability. Early in *Mysticism after modernity*, he argues that most western religious institutions ruled by a group of professionals – "priests, scribes, interpreters, and lawyers" (ibid: 3) – took away from the majority the possibility of personal liberation and happiness in this life and now deliver "only a condition of extreme religious alienation". (ibid) In this context the mystic belongs to an "older charismatic and more democratic tradition, they try to write their way and ours to

a condition of personal happiness. However such writing is dangerous". (ibid) This is why it has tended to be suppressed, banned as he-
retical, outlawed by the ruling minority of clerics, because it is a challenge, however humble and marginal, to the power and legitimacy of
officialdom. As Cupitt puts it, "the mystic was compelled to decon-
struct orthodoxy, and especially the standard doctrine of God, if she
was to achieve personal religious happiness. But if she was found out,
she was burned". (ibid: 4)

Cupitt doesn't provide us with a clear sense of what he means by
"happiness" in this context nor does he supply much evidence to support his contention that this is what mystics aspire to or even place
much emphasis on. It could be argued that personal happiness seems
oddly out of kilter with much mystical literature and practice which
seems intent on dissecting and modifying notions of a personal self in
order to be liberated from its constricting power. Mystics are also
often very keen to point out the dangers of attachment to such notions
of self and to dissolving in some way the *worldly* desires and appetites
which are a manifestation of this deluded self and which tend to lead
to an illusory and unsatisfactory form of happiness.

In another passage Cupitt signals his recognition that unknowing may
be important to mystical practice, but we may also want to question
both the way in which he articulates this point and consider some of
the issues arising indirectly from what he has to say. He writes:

> In Buddhism [...] mysticism is also much more than a protest movement. It is con-
> stitutive of the whole tradition, and in a very special way. The principal cause of
> humanity's prevalent unhappiness is held to be a false construction of the world
> [...] just sitting in meditation, if we persist long enough, will gradually relax us
> and dissolve away the false dualism and the ideas of substance that were troubling
> us. The more everything – including the self – is melted down into a silent out-
> pouring of pure insubstantial secondariness [...] the happier we get to be. (ibid: 5)

A number of points can be made regarding Cupitt's argument in this
passage. Firstly, given that language, particularly verbal language, is
held by many Buddhist thinkers to be one of the major contributors to
the "false construction of the world", it is at least possible that we
have to see language as part of the problem, and to be open to the
possibility that language may be only a part of the web of relations

which constitute reality. Secondly, "sitting in meditation", at least in many Buddhist traditions, is one of the ways in which we attend, *without* verbal commentary or judgement, to the chattering mind as it constantly spins its linguistic construction. Again we couldn't do this if there was nothing other than language. Thirdly, verbal languages, particularly western languages, tend to be agents of dualistic thinking and compartmentalisation, affirming distinction and separateness rather than connection and indivisibility. Finally, the idea of a "silent outpouring of pure insubstantial secondariness" seems curiously at odds with Cupitt's constant affirmation of the idea that there can be nothing outside language (in which case how is silence possible) and surely the term "pure" implies a notion of essence which is, according to Cupitt, precisely the opposite of "secondariness".

As we've seen Cupitt has many interesting things to say about mysticism, particularly about what might be called the politics of religion, that is, the power relations within and around the church as institution, and about the tensions between orthodox and non-orthodox ideas and practices. He argues that mysticism is part of,

> a tradition of protest [...] that is irregular and charismatic, not institutional; it is often lay rather than clerical, and its imagery is almost entirely feminine rather than masculine. Its' typical literary idiom is not law but poetry [...] It seeks personal religious happiness, not by setting up clear distinctions, but rather by dissolving them. (ibid: 82-83)

This is very eloquently expressed, and while I have questioned the way in which Cupitt deploys the term "personal happiness" and what he may mean by it, the position he takes in this passage is one with which many will concur. However, as I've mentioned above there is at times a mismatch between Cupitt's ideas about mysticism and the way in which these ideas are articulated to the reader. This is more than a matter of presentation or style, it suggests, to me at least, that Cupitt finds it difficult to engage with the methods, discourses and meanings of mysticism on their own terms – he seems curiously ill at ease with what mystics say and do. For instance, in the above passage, he appears to be sympathetic to the idea that the imagery of mysticism (as part of the tradition of protest) is "almost entirely feminine" and that "its' typical literary idiom is not law but poetry", yet in his own writing Cupitt is so often very dogmatic, as if he is laying down the law in a very masculine way about the matter in hand. Though mentioned in this passage as an important discourse of the tradition of protest, poetry hardly features in his argument – either as a focus of analysis, point of reference or as a mode of address. Likewise, in a later passage, Cupitt writes:

> The world is created, not by Reason and skill, but by contingency and play. Let it be: let the world make itself. Relativity and play are highly creative, whereas "absolutes" create nothing. Absolutes are utterly useless. They are sterile. (ibid: 95)

The somewhat hectoring, dismissive tone of the latter two sentences, seems out of keeping with the idea that "relativity and play are highly creative". To say that, "absolutes are utterly useless. They are sterile", seems itself to be rather absolutist and extreme. It is also questionable in relation to the evidence: the history of ideas is littered with examples of how a belief in absolutes has, for a time at least, been found to be useful. The huge influence of Plato in the west is surely at least partly due to the attractiveness and usefulness of his philosophy of idealism and absolutism (however much we may disagree with Plato's arguments or with the use to which his ideas have been put).

Perhaps Cupitt's dogmatic rhetoric is only stylistic and we should not read too much into it. However, this may lead us to devalue his expertise as a writer, or to believe that he only adopts this tone as a rhetorical device to stimulate debate and to challenge his readers. Be that as it may, *the way* in which we engage with a subject is surely a manifestation of our thinking about that subject and Cupitt appears to write with the dogmatic certainty of a modernist while espousing a postmodern perspective. Too often his writing has the tenor of a lawyer advocating on behalf of a poet, or perhaps, a sympathetic cleric coming to terms with the writings of a protesting mystic.

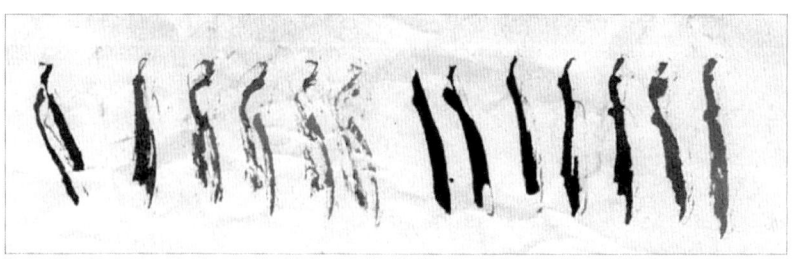

Mysticism, Meister Eckhart, Jacques Derrida and *différance*

In the literature of mysticism we encounter many texts in which the usual conventions of syntax are stretched, questioned and challenged. Many authors seem to be trying to break free of the constraints of orthodox grammar in order to find a signifying equivalence for the feelings, intuitions and thoughts that constitute their particular form of mystical knowledge and experience. Patterns of subversion, inversion, contradiction and paradox, combined with a tendency to develop neologisms and unusual combinations of words, suggest an act of writing that is constantly testing the margins of language, pushing at the limits of *what* can be said and questioning *how* saying and writing can be manifested. Directly or indirectly these authors mount a critique of orthodox vernacular, academic and philosophical discourses, developing a counter-tradition of mystical writings that are then analysed and evaluated by religious institutions and either absorbed into, or excluded from, theological literature.

The challenge that many of these writings pose to established modes of expression and to established religious institutions has prompted numerous acts of inquisition and repression – a catalogue of heresies, exclusions and unimaginable suffering that bears witness to the importance accorded to unorthodox words and thoughts on the part of those in power. This history of linguistic scrutiny, analysis and interpretation, suggests parallels with hermeneutical research in more recent times and with contemporary linguistics and semiology.

Roland Barthes and Jacques Derrida have both made reference to mystical thought and writings at various points in their own work. I'll discuss one such example in relation to Barthes below, but first I'd like to consider Derrida and the relationship between mystical literature and deconstruction.

In his essay, 'Mysticism and transgression: Derrida and Meister Eckhart' (in Silverman 1989), John D. Caputo makes some interesting points about Eckhart's use of language and Derrida's deconstructive enterprise. Caputo argues that Eckhart's importance within the canon of mystical writers is not only because of his ideas about mysticism but more especially because of the way he writes – a way of writing that raises difficulties if we attempt to read it in the same way we might read an academic text, seeking out a rational argument expressed in as concise and clear a manner as possible. Eckhart's writings often seem wilfully obscure, unclear and convoluted. It is as if Eckhart is playing an elaborate game in which one proposition or idea is immediately followed by an assertion that opposes, subverts or questions in some way the previous idea. Each time we think we have grasped a meaning Eckhart pushes the meaning away from us – continually frustrating our attempts to achieve resolution or a sense of completion.

Caputo writes:

> [Eckhart] was constantly altering the syntax of a text, rewriting it so that it said something new. He would fuss with trivial features of a text to which no attention at all had [previously] been paid and make everything turn on them, even to the point of reversing their traditional meaning. (Silverman 1989: 36)

One example, of the many given by Caputo, is the way in which Eckhart reworks and rethinks the Lord's Prayer. Instead of the usual phrase, "thy will be done", Eckhart substitutes these words: "will, become thine". Caputo argues that this is because Eckhart "taught that willing to do God's will is not as high [important] as getting beyond willing altogether". (ibid: 37) Eckhart's wordplay and inventiveness is both deeply disconcerting and liberating, in the way that poetry often is, and it is to poetry that we might turn to find parallels with Eckhart's writing, rather than to traditional philosophy or theology. Eckhart's writing is dynamic. It crackles with the vitality of someone who is excited by spiritual enquiry and seeks to share this excitement, and positive uncertainty, with his readers. This sense of open-ended enquiry is very reminiscent of the practices of sceptics who never reach conclusions, who always have more to find.

Caputo suggests that Eckhart's practice as a writer and thinker anticipates Derrida's ideas of *différance*. Derrida uses this term to denote both the way in which meaning arises in relation to the differences between words, and also the way in which meaning is continually deferred as one word, phrase and sentence is added to another – each succeeding word modifying in some way what has gone before and what follows. In this way a fully resolved meaning is always being postponed or pushed away from us. Thus the reading of any text involves a *process*, an act of negotiating and coming to terms with the endless interplay of word, syntax and interpretation – a process which can never result in a terminal meaning or understanding. For Eckhart this activity is of great importance in that it is a manifestation of his approach to religious thinking and experience – an approach that is about confounding the usual acts of will, desire or intention in relation to God. As Caputo puts it:

> In Eckhart everything turns on *Gelassenheit* (a mainstay of Heidegger's vocabulary) which means letting-be and which includes everything which liberates and sets free. *Gelassenheit* means letting God be God, letting Him be – in yourself, in others, in everything. (ibid: 38)

The term *Gelassenheit* can also be applied to the field of language and meaning, where it may be possible to be freed from the shackles of overly-determined or fixed grammatical structures and predetermined conventional meanings. In this way readers can open up to the destabilising, but exciting, motion and fluidity of language as it is often used by poets and mystics.

In a sense Eckhart's way of writing, which seems so often to generate uncertainty and to frustrate the desire we may have for resolved meanings, is part of a wider strategy to get his readers to free themselves of a dependency on desire and will which, it is hoped, will converge on the goal of religious fulfilment and peace. For Eckhart this is a fallacy. It is the act of willing itself, coming as it does from the limited and conditional self, which limits and conditions a person, so preventing them from entering the open and boundless field of possibility which is God. No statements made about God, or anything else for that matter, can fix the insubstantiality of God (and all things). Words and other sign systems provide only temporary shelters or resting places within the flux of living and making sense.

Barthes, silence and the "speakerly church"

In his book, The Neutral, Roland Barthes has some interesting things
to say about language, power and the relationship between mystical
writings and religious institutions. Barthes refers to "the mystic: the
one who tries to stop language, to suspend its perpetuity; and there he
can only encounter the hostility [...] of the Church". (Barthes 2005:
28) According to Barthes, the Church is "essentially speakerly". (ibid)
He seems to be suggesting that the discourses of mysticism are different to the discourses of the Church, the institution that mediates and
legislates between the individual practitioner of Christianity and the
ineffability of God. Barthes (ibid: 22) argues that "the exercise of
speech, is tied to the problem of power" and the "speakerly" Church is
that place in which theological power resides. The mystic, like the
sceptic (according to Barthes) maintains a silence that embodies or
manifests an emptiness or ineffability that is the domain of God. This
silence, or alternative non-speakerly discourse, sits in a kind of non-
assertive opposition or counter-weight to the Church with all its power, orthodoxy and legislative control over what is thought, said and
written by its members.

Barthes, draws on the writings of Eckhart and Boehme, to discuss the
uneasy relationship between the speakerly Church and the counter-
tradition of mysticism. He suggests that in early Latin a distinction is
made between the two terms: *tacere*, "verbal silence", and *silere*,
"stillness, absent of movement and of noise". (ibid: 21-22) Barthes
associates his own term, the Neutral, with *silere*, the possibility of
keeping silent or still in relation to the jostling movement and competing assertions of the speakerly Church. It is worth quoting Barthes at
length on this issue. Note the notational, enigmatic language he uses, a
poetic discourse deployed throughout the book:

> In short, *silere* would refer to a sort of timeless virginity of things, before they are
> born or after they have disappeared (*silentes* = the dead). This "silence" of nature
> draws near Boehme's mystical vision of God. For Boehme, God "in himself":
> goodness, purity, liberty, silence, eternal light without shadows or oppositions,
> homogenous, "calm and voiceless eternity." However the *silere* of Boehme's God
> makes him unknowable, since *silere* [is] without sign. (ibid: 22)

It is for this reason that God, who cannot manifest Himself, even to Himself, "gives Himself a *contrarium*: a sevenfold 'nature'..." (ibid) This *contrarium*, a dynamic matrix within which the Many arises out of the One, coincides, according to Barthes,

> with the apparition of the Word: there begins language, the act of speaking, the production of speech [...] *tacere* thus, as silence of speech, is opposed to *silere* , as silence of nature or of divinity; then [...] the two equalize, become synonyms, but to the benefit of *tacere*: nature is so to speak sacrificed to speech: there is no longer silence outside speech [...] "Everything was silent". (ibid)

Barthes' train of thought is not particularly easy to follow here, but as far as I understand him he is suggesting that speech, and any claims of a right to speak, arise out of the quandary that God, who is "without sign" and "unknowable", a silent divine entity, can only be actualised (at least in relation to the human sphere) by manifesting a *contrarium*, a place in which the divine *contra-diction* between positive/negative, presence/absence, known/unknown, word/ineffability, can be played out within the compass of human experience. But the *contrarium* is not a place or state in which we feel at ease. We resolve the contradiction by taking sides, coming down in favour of one assertion or another – either/or – and in this case we come down on the side of speech, the Positive. Thus in the social and political sphere, for instance, we assert the right to speak rather than to be silent, and we speak on behalf of the human, not on behalf of nature or the divine. According to Barthes the ecological movement signals a growing recognition of "the right to nature's peacefulness, the right to *silere*". (ibid: 23)

For Barthes, *silere*, the silence of nature and God, is something to which the mystic is drawn and to which the sceptic aspires. While the sceptic suspends belief and judgement in relation to all assertions, maintaining a silence in regard to defining what is true while continuing to investigate, the mystic is "one who tries to stop language" (ibid: 28) in order to enter the house of God. In so doing the mystic often upsets the church, the surrogate house of God, by exercising silence when the Church calls for speech, assertion, debate and judgement. Barthes connects *silere* with the non-verbal strategies employed by Zen teachers and the Daoist belief that, "he who knows the Dao speaks not, he who speaks knows not". (ibid)

Positive absence

Another contemporary view of mysticism is put forward by Jean-Luc Marion in his introduction to a collection of essays by various authors, *Mystics: Presence and Aporia.* (ed. Kessler & Sheppard 2004) Marion argues that in an era when many consider metaphysics to be no longer tenable as a philosophical pursuit we have to construct an approach to mysticism that doesn't necessarily centre upon an experiential relationship to an ontological or metaphysical reality. Marion argues that if we are to discuss mysticism in a rational scientific way (which seems to be his intention), then we have to attend to manifestations of mysticism as objects of scientific enquiry. His way of doing this is to accept that "mystical phenomena" are characterised by having an "uncontrollable excess of intuition within them, above and beyond all of the meanings that we will ever be able to assign them". (ibid: 3) This seems an odd way to phrase his point, given that it is difficult to see how intuitions can reside *within* phenomena – surely intuitions are a way of apprehending or experiencing phenomena? However, Marion goes on to suggest that such phenomena "bedazzle the gaze" with the intensity of their radiance. (ibid) Marion uses the term, "saturated phenomena" to denote these mystical events or occurrences: "saturated phenomena, appear, as if in opposition to our experience. We shall therefore also call them paradoxes or counterphenomena". (ibid)

Marion argues for a variant on the apophatic/kataphatic dialectic [see p. 49 above] – the oscillating dynamic of speaking and being silent, saying and not-saying:

> according to the Greek fathers [...] God is invisible, unspeakable, uncircumscriba-
> ble, and incomprehensible. Yet the experience of not being able to comprehend,
> see, or think God can be taken seriously as a positive experience. We can be con-
> fronted by something completely outside of our reach and nevertheless present as
> such, as absent. (ibid: 4)

Marion argues that this idea of positive absence can be found in Gregory of Nyssa: "What we have to see is the very fact not to see"; (ibid) a phrase also used by Dionysius' in his *Mystical Theology*; and Thomas Aquinas has this variant: "the ultimate point of the human knowledge about God is to know that we don't know God". (ibid) Marion then refers to Wittgenstein's enigmatic ending to the *Tracta-*

tus: "What we cannot speak about we must pass over in silence". (ibid – Marion's version of Wittgenstein's sentence) But, as Marion points out, there are different modes of silence:

> We may keep silent in such a way that we refuse to think about a thing, refrain from thinking it, and take it to be kept outside the horizon of our thought. But there is another way to remain silent, which is to worship, to take a thing so seriously that we have only one way to speak about it, which is precisely to keep silent. (ibid)

R.S. Thomas, presence and absence

The Welsh poet R.S. Thomas, who died in 2000, was an overtly religious writer whose poetry can be read as a record of spiritual enquiry – a search for an elusive God, in which absence seems to be as significant as presence. In poem after poem Thomas interrogates the silence and emptiness which God manifests or in which God resides – like a rare tree in a desert.

For most Christians God is personified, *He* is given attributes, intentions and actions. God seems to be made in the image of man. But, as D.Z. Phillips (1986: 82) points out, we use, in law, another way of thinking about God when we refer to *acts of God*, meaning events that seem to have no agency or intention behind them (for example, lightning strikes, floods, freak acts of nature, and accidents). In these cases there is an absence *at work*, so to speak, an absence of intention or volition. In a similar way we can think of God as an absence – *Deus Absconditus*. We can approach this God, or at least come to a positive unknowing of this God through what, in the literature of mysticism, is called a *via negativa* – a path of negation.

If God is an absence, we are more likely to find God by giving up our intention to search, or we are more likely to enter a state of Godliness by giving up our intentional, wilful self – emptying ourselves of those qualities which in their fullness divide us from God. It seems to Thomas that God at times participates in a reciprocal emptying or giving up. As Phillips puts it: "A dying to the self is at the heart of the Godhead [...] God empties himself of power in making room for man". (ibid: 83) For Thomas, the universe and everything that happens in it can be seen as a manifestation of God's grace, existing without reference to human intention or reason. According to Phillips, the man "who sees the givenness of his life as an act of grace, has come to a knowledge of God", (ibid) or at least, we might say, to the possibility of such knowledge.

Thomas writes from a position of belief in a God-given, not a human-centred, universe. Phillips argues that this leads to a paradoxical situation:

> The sheer givenness of things speaks of an absence to the poet. By seeing grace in all things, the giver of grace cannot be seen as a thing alongside those that are given. Such an experience of a presence mediated through absence, God making all the difference to the world because he cannot be in it alongside all other things, comes to the poet. (ibid: 106)

From this perspective, in the act of giving, God removes himself from that which is given. The giver cannot be the given. God is thus always outside the universe even though his grace is all-pervasive. This paradox is analysed, explored and grappled with by Thomas. The idea of presence in absence and absence in presence, acts as a kind of *koan* [see p. 127] – an insoluble puzzle over which the poet ponders throughout his long life. Indeed paradoxes and contradictions are found, both as characteristics and compositional devices, in a great many of Thomas's poems. For example, God is like a rare bird, but, as Thomas writes in *Sea-watching*, "a rare bird is / rare. It is when one is not looking, / at times one is not there / that it comes". (Thomas 2001: 306) In *The Flower*, he refers to "the rainbow of your coming and going" – though he is speaking about a flower he could as easily be speaking of God. (ibid: 280) Thomas maps such comings and goings with clinical precision, accepting that for most of the time God is intangible, just out of reach and seemingly indifferent to human affairs. In the poem, *Near and Far*, God is spoken of as being, "always as far off / as you are near, terrifying / me as much by your proximity / as by your being light-years away". (Thomas 2004: 250) This oscillating sense of God, as here then not here, close enough to burn us then as far away as an icy star, energises Thomas's poetry and gives a dynamic tension to his poetic voice.

God's otherness, indifference and ineffableness are noted in many poems, almost in passing. Thomas seems resigned to the fact that he seeks but can never find, knocking on a door that remains firmly shut or tantalisingly slightly ajar. He accepts that God is indeterminate and beyond human understanding. He acknowledges that God is beyond, or before, what can be said, and God's dominion, the whole universe, is implacably mute, resisting all attempts at description, categorisation and definition. The poet hurls his words at the sky, only to be answered by a strange and bewildering cloud. Yet it is in this strange and bewildering world, God's gift, in which Thomas sometimes finds solace and consolation. But the consolation is usually short-lived or has a sting in the tail, as Thomas notes in, *Praise*, where he writes of God "answering our most complex / prayers with the simplicity / of a flower" – a much-used, even clichéd image. But then the poet seems to change gear and the image of the gentle flower is followed by a more disturbing thought: that just when "we would domesticate you [God] / to our uses" you confront us "with the rioting / viruses under our lens". (in Phillips 1986: 109)

For Thomas, life is a struggle to find or construct meaning, a striving to come to terms with the contradictions inherent in a belief that God is full of grace but seemingly hidden and out of reach. In the aptly named poem, The Combat, we find this conundrum eloquently expressed. The whole poem appears to be addressed to God (as are many of Thomas's works) and it opens with the blunt assertion: "You have no name", followed by a description of how "we wrestled with you all / day" only to find that "you withdraw, leaving us nursing / our bruises, our dislocations". The second stanza is worth quoting in its entirety as a concise statement of Thomas's poetic and religious credo:

> For the failure of language
> there is no redress. The physicists
> tell us your size, the chemists
> the ingredients of your
> thinking. But who you are
> does not appear, nor why
> on the innocent marches
> of vocabulary you should choose
> to engage us, belabouring us
> with your silence. We die, we die
> with the knowledge that your resistance
> is endless at the frontier of the great poem.
> (Thomas 2001: 291)

Thomas presents us with a contemporary example of a mysticism of transcendence – the poet seeking to be aware of, and to engage with, a transcendent order that is always resistant to human cognition. Though we may find it hard to go along with Thomas's belief in a transcendent God, we can still find much that is rewarding and illuminating in his poetry. Particularly his ideas about the otherness of nature, the implacable indifference of a world that exists regardless of our attention, an *outside* that constantly challenges our attempts to tame, name and classify it. Paradoxical as it may seem he attends to this world with an intensity that is both deeply engaged yet benignly indifferent, he subjects everything he encounters to forensic scrutiny – be it the world of human affairs and feelings, or the natural world around him. Thomas was a keen bird-watcher and it seems to me that this is indicative of his approach to all things: precise and curious; passionate and unsentimentally observant.

Poetry as bone, beyond understanding

In the introduction to his anthology of contemporary poetry, Conductors of Chaos, Iain Sinclair writes about poetry as a remainder, a leftover, "Poetry will always be that splinter of bone that is left when the rest of the skeleton has been devoured". He also argues that there may be something strange about it, something that is always at a distance and resistant to conventional notions of intelligibility or meaningfulness, "The work I value is that which seems most remote, alienated, fractured. I don't claim to 'understand' it but I like having it around". (Sinclair 1996: xvii)

Stepping around the self – Simone Weil (1909-1943)

In this section I'm going to discuss some of the ideas of Simone Weil, drawing particularly on Weil's text, Gravity and Grace, in the translation by Emma Crawford and Marion von der Ruhr (Weil 2002) and the poet Anne Carson's writing about Weil in her book, *Decreation*. (2006: 167-170) Weil was born in Paris in 1909, and died of tuberculosis in England in 1943, aged only thirty-four. She seems to have been a precocious child, apparently proficient in Greek by the time she was twelve years old. She is well-known for her writings on philosophy, politics and mysticism – most of which were published posthumously.

Weil's writing in Gravity and Grace is often enigmatic and her meaning can be hard to fathom. The book consists of a series of enigmatic assertions, almost a catalogue of unsolvable puzzles that challenge the reader's ability to interpret and make sense. With Carson's help I will do my best to say something about Weil's ideas about the self and how the self can be an impediment to encountering God.

Weil makes use of the term "decreation", a neologism that she never explicitly defines but which seems to denote the intentional dissolving of the subjective ego – what Weil also refers to as the "social *ego*" and the "psychological *ego*". (Weil 2002: 33) In Weil's view, the subjective ego is a very limited and limiting construct that prevents us from experiencing the fullness of Being – it "blocks God's light". (in Carson 2006: 167) Weil seems to equate God with Being and Being with God. She argues that God who is infinite, gives up his infinitude in order to allow other beings, particularly human beings, to exist. In an act of reciprocation human beings have to give up their finite being, the "psychological *ego*" in order to be re-united with God, to experience Being in its fullest sense – what she refers to as the "uncreated". (Weil 2002: 32) She writes, "In a sense God renounces being everything. We should renounce being something". (ibid: 33) She goes on, "every time we raise the *ego* [...] as high as we raise it, we degrade ourselves to an infinite degree by confining ourselves to being no more than that. When the *ego* is abased [...] we know that we are not that". (ibid) In a typically paradoxical phrase she suggests that, "we only possess what we renounce". (ibid: 34) In other words we can only realise the full potential of our being by giving back to God what has been given to us, that is, the ego-self. "We possess nothing in this world other than the power to say 'I'. This is what we must yield up to God". (in Carson 2006: 167) Somehow we have to step aside in our ego-centred being in order to encounter God or Being – in the sense of being fully integrated into the relational universe.

This idea of self-surrender is found throughout the literature of mysticism in both Christian and Islamic traditions. To the extent that we are present in the world as an ego-centred self we cannot be fully present, fully alive and we cannot participate in the world because we feel ourselves to be cut off from the rest of the world. Weil writes plaintively, "if only I could see a landscape as it is when I am not there. But when I am in any place I disturb the silence of heaven by the beating of my heart". (in Carson 2006: 169) As far as Weil is concerned [like Jacob Boehme, see p. 33 above] we cannot perceive or engage with the universe as it is, in its relational state, if we are bound within an ego-centred self that is a distortion or shrunken form of what we actually are. The noise of our monkey mind, the chattering ego, prevents us from perceiving the full spectrum of sensations that weaves us into the world. To attend fully to the phenomenal field, to be here in the fullest sense, we have to find a way to open up and transform the ego-centred, impermeable self, into a more porous self, the relational self – a current of being within the relational universe.

Writing at the end of her life (she died of tuberculosis in London in 1943) Weil argues for her own very distinctive approach to philosophy. Although her thinking continues the tradition of Plato and is characterised as "transcendentalist", Weil is against dogmatism and turns upside-down some of the positivist assumptions of the male philosophical canon. For Weil, philosophy depends upon the cultivation of humility and a sense of unknowing, combined with an open-ended sense of enquiry or curiosity. When the limits of what is known by philosophical analysis and rational enquiry are reached, we must not turn away, but continue to be attentive, to face the margins of the known in a patient and contemplative state. Weil writes,

> There is no entry into the transcendent until the human faculties – intelligence, will, human love – have come up against a limit, and the human being waits at this threshold, which he can make no move to cross, without turning away and without knowing what he wants, in fixed, unwavering attention. (Weil 1970: 335)

This idea of philosophy as selfless enquiry and contemplative attention is a direct development of her mystical experience and thought. She sums up her views in the following way:

> The proper method of philosophy consists in clearly conceiving the insoluble problems in all their insolubility and then in simply contemplating them, fixedly and tirelessly, year after year, without any hope, patiently waiting. (ibid)

As Weil herself acknowledges seen from this perspective and "by this standard, there are few philosophers". (ibid) For Weil philosophy involves both rational cognition, articulated in logical argument and academic discourse, but it also involves an experiential enquiry, often at the margins of rational thought, that can only be articulated in a more allusive, poetic and paradoxical language. There are echoes here of the beliefs and methods of other mystical writers, from the anonymous author of the Cloud of Unknowing, to Teresa of Avila and Meister Eckhart.

Observation V – being here

Over the hills behind our old house there's a Cistercian monastery, an imposing collection of granite buildings clustered around a church – all of it built by a handful of monks between the early 1840s and 1939, when the church was completed. Surrounding the monastery is a farm run by the monks, mostly Friesian cattle, some fields of turnips and other crops and hay fields providing winter fodder for the stock. The abbot occasionally had dealings with my Dad, who managed a large granite quarry on land adjacent to the monastery. When I was a boy an old monk, Father Vincent, used to visit us from time-to-time, stopping-off on his long slow walks around the lanes and open moorland behind our house. I remember his visits. He would sit in our kitchen sipping tea from a mug while my mother chatted with him. There was always a slight air of reverent embarrassment as my mother tried to think of things to say. He didn't speak much. He wore an old grey coat over his pale, thickly-woven habit. On his feet he had thick woollen socks and heavy sandals that were always scuffed with mud. Tiny spikes of grass or straw clung to his clothes and his bare head.

For some reason I loved to see him in our kitchen. I can't remember if I ever spoke to him or he to me. But I was entranced by his sturdy appearance, his quietness and the way he lifted his mug of tea as if it was a chalice of communion wine. It was as if every gesture of his body and every word he uttered *mattered*. Not that he was pompous or self-regarding, in fact he was very unassuming and straightforward, more like the farm workers I knew than a vicar. But he had a gentle gravity, a presence, a condensed way of being that radiated around him. It wasn't a holy aura or anything like that. And he wasn't stern or serious, far from it. He had a wry smile and a chuckle that seemed always about to burst into roaring laughter. Whenever I heard this reassuring sound it made me realise no matter how mad life could be (and madness never seemed far away) all would be well. It was as if everything in our kitchen became more sharply defined when he was in the room. He was mindful, relaxed, yet very intense. He seemed more alive than we were, although when he was with us I also felt more alive. When he spoke he used words as if he was building something with them. It made me think of the monks I'd often seen repairing the dry-stone walls around their fields, carefully lifting and turning heavy pieces of granite to find the best fit. His sentences were short, pithy and workmanlike, but they seemed to say so much.

Like my grandfather and a few other individuals I've encountered here and there, he showed me how life can be lived with humility, with extreme economy of mind and language, and with irrepressible good humour. He was a Bodhisattva, a compassionate guide, and it was hard to accept his absence when I heard from my mother that he was too old to walk the hills any more.

Silhouette: Martin Buber

even if it was hell   nothing at all   only everything
where is there room for it to unfold, to present itself?
the relation is all   the relationship is everything, of
which there is no thing, and nothing else   when the
actual is all, there is no other   it is a difficult reading,
the reading of what is   there is no translation, only
a pointing & a recognition & a retelling & an opening
to it all…

only to glimpse, to be familiar
yet to be witness to the strangeness
of things as they are – the carpet
now illumined by patches of light
and moving shadows that trace the
breeze outside

only the acceptance of the presence is required… and only
when we are present is the word decomposed &
revealed as another…

we can only
witness, there is

nothing more,
or less,
to be done…

[Reading Buber's, *I and Thou*]

Part III

Scepticism

"The sceptic's end is quietude in respect
of matters of opinion and moderate feeling
in respect of things unavoidable".
(Sextus Empiricus 1990: 23)

"We hang like clouds between heaven and earth,
between something and nothing".
(Wright 2001: 89)

Introduction – what is scepticism?

As with mysticism, scepticism comprises a heterogeneous body of writings, oral statements, beliefs, practices and states of consciousness. A deeply sceptical tendency or disposition can be found in the work of: Pyrrho of Elis, Sextus Empiricus, Spinoza, David Hume, Ludwig Wittgenstein, John Dewey, Richard Rorty, Paul Ricoeur and other exponents of hermeneutics, Roland Barthes and Umberto Eco. This current of ideas can be seen as a counter-tradition to the dogmatism of many mainstream western philosophers.

It may be argued that to discuss scepticism in relation to mysticism is not to compare like with like, for the main focus of sceptical enquiry is knowledge and the main concerns of mysticism are matters like being, consciousness or God. This is undoubtedly true. Sceptics pay attention to questions like: what is knowledge? what is it to believe one thing rather than another? what is it to claim that a particular statement is true? is it reasonable to be certain that one's views about the world are correct? and so on. These are the kinds of problems to which Pyrrho and Sextus Empiricus devote themselves, developing methods of analysis which, as we shall see, dig up much of the ground for certainty upon which we base our beliefs. However, we shall also see that the underlying purpose of these methods of analysis and deconstruction is to achieve a state of equanimity – peace of mind – to live life less troubled by many of the worries and dissatisfactions that affect us. While the focus of sceptical methods and discourse is upon knowledge and beliefs about knowledge, the *aim* is to bring about a change in our experience of life and in our state of mind or consciousness. In this sense at least there is some overlap between scepticism and mysticism.

Scepticism and dogmatism

It could be argued that the main impetus for the development of scepticism in early Greek culture was as a counter to the development of philosophical and proto-scientific claims about the nature of reality – propositions about the world that seemed to explain the workings of the world and gave human beings a sense of certainty about knowledge. This sense of certainty went hand-in-hand with a belief that clear distinctions could be made between true statements and false ones and by implication that actions based on such true or false statements could be considered as being right or wrong – well-founded or wrong-headed. This belief that knowledge can be certain (or true) tended to give rise to a belief that judgements can also be certain, definite and right. Sadly, and it is not clear to me why, these beliefs are nearly always accompanied by a tendency to assume that alternative views or judgements must be false or wrong. The idea that there might be a number of different truths or ethical positions that may be equally valid seems so often to be incompatible with certainty about one's own views. This sense of certainty about knowledge and judgement is what the early sceptics like Pyrrho found to be problematic and potentially dangerous.

The sceptics referred to this sense of certainty as dogmatism and they encountered manifestations of dogmatic thinking all around them, but especially in the many schools of philosophy that characterised the Hellenistic age (c. 323-30 BCE) – the age of the Stoics, the Epicureans, various followers of Plato and Aristotle, and the sceptics themselves. This was an age united by a strengthening belief in rationalism, though also marked by a tension between the rise of materialism and empiricism (important to the Stoics and Epicureans) and the various kinds of idealism and immaterialism still espoused by the followers of Plato and Aristotle. The sceptics raised doubts about all claims to knowledge and about all dogmatic assertions that one method, belief or value was intrinsically correct, true or dependable. Indeed, the sceptics argued that it was the dependence upon such claims that prevented the dogmatist from achieving a state of equanimity or inner peace (*ataraxia*). [see below]

Sceptical dialectics

Some of the earliest manifestations of the sceptical tradition are ascribed to Pyrrho of Elis (c.360-c.275BC) – as articulated by his student Timon, (c.315-c.225) and by Sextus Empiricus, who probably wrote his *Outlines of Pyrrhonism* during the second or third centuries AD. It is important to recognise that scepticism seems to have been intended as much as a way of living as a mode of philosophical analysis and discourse. The practice of scepticism was seen as a way of achieving equanimity, a way of avoiding the conflict, disturbance and pain associated with attaching oneself to doctrines and opinions that were always open to equal and opposing arguments.

As far as we can tell from Timon and Sextus, Pyrrho employed a dialectical method not dissimilar to that of Socrates. All philosophical assertions were subjected to careful scrutiny. Statements were analysed in a logical manner in order to reveal underlying weaknesses, inconsistencies and contradictions. Reason was used as a forensic tool to dissect the most obvious truth or dogma until what had seemed reasonable and self-evident was shown to be unreasonable, inconclusive or open to many, often contradictory, interpretations. According to Thomas McEvilley the Pyrrhonists used the dialectical method as,

> an antilinguistic or anticonceptual force that would blow away what the Cynics called the smoke or mist of opinions and value judgments and restore attention to phenomena in themselves (McEvilley 2002: 420)

Through dialectical analysis *all* opinions are shown to be relative and conditional, full of distortions, imbalances and partialities:

> The study of counterarguments to one's own opinions was meant, according to Sextus, to lead to a general state of *epoché*, 'suspension of belief,' which could in turn lead to a state of inner freedom from the domination of linguistic categories

(*aphasia*), which in turn will steady into an effective balance (*arrepsia*) which is naturally and effortlessly followed by a state of imperturbability (*ataraxia*). (ibid)

Although the sceptics can be seen as in a way discrediting any notion that true assertions can be made about anything, their analytical dialectics, the constant deployment of counter-arguments, leads them to the realisation that in different contexts opposite assertions may be equally true. Therefore to assert any proposition as being true or false, positive or negative, right or wrong, is to be in error. Dogmatic assertions of any kind are to be avoided.

From a sceptical point of view human history can be seen as being littered with conflicts fought in the name of dogmatic truths, or false certainties, of every persuasion. If we are to be free of error, to be free "of the domination of linguistic categories" we have to be open to the indeterminacy of things, the awareness that all things are without essence or self-existence. This state of actuality, the sceptics refer to as *aoristia*, "lack of boundary or definition". This is very similar to Adorno's "non-identity" [see p. 155] and to what Buddhists refer to as *sunyata*, or "emptiness". McEvilley points out that the indeterminacy of things makes them ungraspable in epistemological terms. We cannot define or categorise or assign truth-values to what is indeterminate and indefinable. This ungraspable, ineffableness is what the sceptics call *akatalepsia*. (ibid: 458)

Observation VI – the shower

Reef Hotel, Zanzibar, 1997. From the head of the shower a thin stream of speckled light falls to the concrete floor – a rib of water arced against the dark swaying lattice of palm trees. Ants dart here and there to drink from the wet concrete, eventually skittering back to the dusty margins of dry grass. In the arc of light I can see myself and the room and the view beyond the window – all of it shimmering with the same watery rhythm.

Sceptical enquiry

Julia Annas (2000) argues that it is important to clarify the meaning of the term "sceptic" and to separate out its popular negative associations from the Greek philosophical traditions that provide us with the word.

> The Greek term *skepticos* means, not a negative doubter, but an investigator, someone going in for *skeptesthai* or enquiry. As the late sceptic author Sextus Empiricus puts it, there are dogmatic philosophers, who think that they have found the truth; negative dogmatists, who feel entitled to the position that the truth cannot be found; and the sceptics, who are unlike both the other groups in that they are not committed either way. They are still investigating things. (Annas 2000: 69)

This undecidability or indeterminacy regarding notions of truth is a fundamental characteristic of the sceptical approach, particularly as articulated by Sextus Empiricus. Enquiry is always open-ended, knowledge is always revisible, subject to changing experiences and the flux of life. According to the sceptics:

> Real enquiry, thorough investigation, will reveal that the situation was more complex and problematic; we turn out never to have reason to commit ourselves one way or the other, and so end up suspending judgment – that is, having a detached and uncommitted attitude – to whatever the issue was. (Annas 2000: 69-70)

There are echoes here of Derrida's use of the idea of *undecidability*. A number of authors, including Dreyfus (2003:241-245) have also argued for the similarities between deconstruction and the dialectics of scepticism, Madhyamika Buddhism or mystics like Meister Eckhart (eg. Caputo 1989: 24-39). It is also possible to identify affinities between the sceptical emphasis on open-ended enquiry and the ideas of John Dewey, as articulated in his book, *Art as Experience*, first published in 1934. Richard Shusterman (1993: 3) argues that,

> In Dewey's pragmatism, experience rather than truth is the final standard... His instrumental theory of knowledge sees the ultimate aim of all inquiry, scientific or aesthetic, not as mere truth or knowledge itself but as better experience or experienced value...

Dewey puts forward the notion that the arts, like the sciences and philosophy, are agencies of enquiry, criticism and enrichment, functioning within the continuum of experience. He suggests that enhancing the quality of experience is, or should be, a primary concern for art, science and philosophy. For Dewey these modes of enquiry and imagining are integral to human living.

Dynamic equanimity and non-attachment to dogmas

By avoiding dogmatic adherence to either side in an argument, by suspending judgement and belief, sceptics can develop an attitude of continuing enquiry and openness to all possibilities. The equanimity that is said to accompany this open-ended enquiry is dynamic and intellectually playful, characterised by a suppleness, fluidity and openness of mind. Tolerance and even-handed acknowledgement of diversity and difference seem to be consequences of the skilful use of sceptical methods – a marked alternative to the entrenchments of dogmatic attachment to particular beliefs and values.

Just as Buddhist teachings [see Part IV] include a recognition of the dangers of attachment to ideas of non-attachment, so the sceptics point to the need not to become attached to the idea that suspension of judgement, *epoché, will* produce quietude, *ataraxia.* As Terence Penelhum (1983: 289) points out, *ataraxia* follows "as if by chance" from the suspension of judgement and belief, it is not something to be gained by a dogmatic expectation that it will happen as a result of such a belief. Not only are there echoes of Buddhist thinking here, but also Daoist notions of *wu-wei,* doing by not-doing – acting against the flow or way of nature.

Just as Buddhists and Daoists don't imagine that skilful exercising of non-attachment will somehow leave us free from physical pain, or no longer be subject to cold or other wholly natural sensations, so sceptics recognise that *ataraxia* does not free us from such sensations. Penelhum (ibid: 290) quotes Sextus: "we do not suppose, however, that the skeptic is wholly untroubled; but we say that he is troubled by things unavoidable; for we grant that he is cold at times and thirsty." Sextus argues that while sceptics are affected, as everyone is, by unavoidable conditions and circumstances, at least they are not also affected by the disappointment and anxiety caused by a belief that such conditions are either bad or evil, or that they should be avoidable by one method or another. It is adherence to this fallacious and unnecessary belief that leads to dissatisfaction and distress, as it is inevitably contradicted by the course of events in any one's life. The sceptic is therefore able to experience such conditions and be only moderately affected by them – he or she feels the cold but doesn't experience additional layers of regret, disappointment or bitterness that somehow we *shouldn't be feeling cold.*

Observation VII –learning from the lizard

In a room in an old house in the south of France a lizard is curled around the vertical pipe entering one end of a cast-iron radiator. The pipe is warm. The room is cool, outside it is cold. A wintry wind still blows, scratching at the opening flower buds on the small almond tree out in the courtyard. It is early April, at the beginning of a spring that has been harried from day to day by a winter that is loath to say goodbye. The lizard has been here all day, gathering warmth into his sleek mottled body. When we move he watches us, alert to every movement in the room. While we are restless, hoping for a change in the weather, the lizard seems at ease, unhurriedly attentive and very patient.

David Hume's "mitigated scepticism"

We can link the recognition by sceptics that a wholly untroubled life is probably impossible to some of the ideas of the eighteenth-century Scottish philosopher, David Hume. According to one influential interpreter of Hume's ideas, John Passmore, Hume argues "that it is completely impossible for any human being constantly to maintain a totally sceptical position [...] One cannot *live* as a total sceptic". (in Magee 1987: 153) However, as Passmore points out, it *is useful* to pursue a sceptical argument to its conclusions, not in order to sweep away all beliefs and rational evidence for beliefs, but in order to sweep away the illusion that we can be certain that our beliefs can be based upon rational argument and can thus have any degree of certainty attached to them. It is this sense of certainty in the truth or evidential justification that Hume argues against.

Passmore suggests that what Hume is proposing is what he calls "a mitigated scepticism" – the effect of which is to lead us to recognise

> just how little can be established [as true or certain and thus to] free ourselves from any kind of dogmatism [...] that attitude of mind which the eighteenth century called 'enthusiasm' and we call 'fanaticism' [...] the belief that there are truths which can be established in such a manner that anyone who fails to recognise them must be morally wicked and can therefore properly be exterminated". (ibid: 154)

In other words Hume's sceptical dialectic is a tool with which to dismantle false certainties. If he were alive today Hume would probably consider fundamentalism, whether religious or political, as a very pernicious form of dogmatism, to be dissected and dismembered using the tools of sceptical argument.

Passmore (ibid) reminds us that "Hume rejects the possibility of constructing large metaphysical systems", precisely because all systems can be shown to be flawed in terms of consistency of construction and/or as being built upon unreliable assumptions and beliefs. Hume is a very effective observer of human hubris and sees this as being particularly evident in relation to our unwarranted certainty in the truth or rightness (righteousness) of our belief in one political, social or religious system or another – this unwarranted certainty he classed as superstition and, according to Passmore, it is superstition against which his philosophy is principally directed. (ibid)

"Skeptical fideism"

In arguing that there can be a close connection between mysticism and scepticism it is useful to consider the widely recognised link between sceptical methods of enquiry and argumentation and aspects of Christian theology. Terence Penelhum (1983: 287-318) uses the term "skeptical fideism" to refer to "a tradition which tries to enlist the doubts and questions of the philosophical sceptic in the supposed interests of Christian faith". (ibid: 288) Exponents of this approach might include: Montaigne, Erasmus, Bayle, Pascal and Kierkegaard. We can perceive in the thinking of each of these writers an attempt to reconcile Christian faith and experience with a sceptical mode of enquiry and argumentation. They are also deeply critical of theological dogmatism and expose faulty reasoning and misguided assumptions to the light of careful scrutiny.

It is worth quoting Penelhum at length on this matter:

> Skeptical Fideists saw themselves in opposition to radical enthusiasts, and believed humility and intellectual self-depreciation to be an urgent Christian need. [....] the stances of faith and of Skepticism are [....] similar in certain respects. Both involve dissatisfaction with the disturbance and anxiety associated with the commitments of the world of secular common sense. Both recommend, as a cure for these anxieties, not physical disengagement from the commonsense world, but a kind of participation in it that requires inner detachment or otherness from it. (ibid: 297)

In opposing "radical enthusiasts" Penelhum's Skeptical Fideists echo Hume's opposition to "enthusiasm" and "superstition". While Hume argues against all attempts to construct metaphysical systems, including religious systems, because they can always be shown to be riddled with inconsistency, false assumptions and misguided beliefs, Skeptical Fideists, like Pascal and Kierkegaard, seek to mitigate the excessive dogmatism of the established church and to acknowledge in their religious practice the pivotal role of doubt and uncertainty. This integration of doubt and faith, certainty and uncertainty, within a religious context can be seen as an example of what Nicholas of Cusa refers to as the "coincidence of opposites". (see McFarlane 2004)

Michel de Montaigne, scepticism and God

In his longest essay, An Apology for Raymond Sebond, Michel de Montaigne not only explains and defends the natural theology espoused by the Castilian writer, Raymond Sebond, he also articulates his understanding of, and support for, Pyrrhonist scepticism. Indeed his essay, published in 1580, is one of the first to take full account of the thinking of Pyrrho and Sextus Empiricus since the publication in France in 1562 of the first modern edition of Sextus', Outlines of Pyrrhonism.

Montaigne's essays, including the Apology, present us with a lucid record of continuous enquiry, a testimony of apparently endless curiosity and questioning. Over and over again Montaigne defers making up his mind about particular ideas and issues. He is always investigating and rarely definite in his conclusions. Indeed the idea of a conclusion seems anathema to his dialectical method and to his inquisitive mentality. He reminds us that he has taken for his own emblem an image of a balance with the words, "what do I know", inscribed on it. (Montaigne 1993: 100) And it is the interweaving of doubting curiosity, balanced opinions and open-mindedness that animates Montaigne's thinking.

Montaigne seems to approve of the Pyrrhonist strategy of not taking sides, of maintaining neutrality in relation to the different sides of an argument. He acknowledges that dogmatic certainty in relation to any opinion, positive or negative, so often leads to trouble, to argument and conflict. He notes how "the senses deceive our intellect; it deceives them in their turn". (1993: 179) He goes on, "Quarrels are constantly arising because one person hears, sees or tastes something differently from another. As much as anything, we quarrel over the diversity of the images conveyed to us by our senses". (ibid: 183) Recognising that the diversity of images is inevitable, just as a diversity of opinions, beliefs and values will always arise in relation to any aspect of human affairs, he agrees with Sextus that it is folly to attach oneself to any one image, taste, belief or opinion, if by that we mean that we consider our choice to be the right or true one and others to be wrong or untrue.

To read Montaigne's essay, is to engage with the equivocations of a mind that interrogates religious belief in order to see more clearly what a belief in God might mean to a rational, intelligent person. Montaigne sifts through the grains of Catholicism as it presents itself to him, finding that much of it is chaff, though some of it may be nourishing wheat. Throughout the Apology he presents us with countless beliefs, habits of thought and moral codes, only to show how they are insubstantial, fallacious or contradictory. He scrutinises assumptions and dogmas in such a way that we can see the inconsistencies in them. He does this in a spirit of open-ended enquiry, laced with a humane wonder at the comic folly of human belief and gullibility. Montaigne's forensic analysis of his own personality reveals a ragged patchwork of thoughts, emotions, sensations and attachments that are anything but homogeneous and consistent. His scepticism finds little room for certainty and no room for any absolutes other than God, an entity that remains enigmatic and ineffable, and towards which Montaigne seems equivocal. It is as if God is that which remains when all the trappings of belief, ritual, dogma and convention have been removed from the religious institutions that made up the Catholic church of his time. God is a remainder, a possibility leftover from the exercise of doubt and critical enquiry.

In a way that is perhaps surprising, Montaigne argues for the efficacy of Pyrrhonist scepticism, as a preparation for Christian practice. He makes a leap, which many of his sceptic forebears might have considered a leap too far, from sceptical enquiry and doubt to Christian belief of a particular kind. He maintains that the sceptical method can lead us to become open to divine grace: "Man, stripped of all human learning [is] all the more able to lodge the divine within him." He then uses the arresting phrase, "annihilating his intellect to make room for faith." (ibid: 74) Montaigne is a sceptical Christian and however much we may catch a scent of inconsistency in his thinking, he seems to see nothing illogical in arguing that the dialectical tools developed by Pyrrho and Sextus can be used to strip away false certainties, beliefs and dogmas in order to open the human mind and heart to something other, a potential for another kind of knowledge or experience. Once we are free of attachment to one side or the other in the conflict of dogmatic assertions, we may become "a blank writing-tablet, made ready for the finger of God to carve such letters on [us] as he pleases." (ibid) This may seem a strange step for Montaigne to take in his seemingly remorseless exercise of sceptical logic, but it is important to give due consideration to his argument.

Montaigne accepts, indeed he seems to celebrate, the bounded and provisional qualities of human understanding. We may seek transcendence but we cannot avoid our limitations. At the end of the Apology he quotes Seneca: "Oh, what a vile and abject thing is man if he does not rise above humanity." (ibid: 189) But he immediately goes on to write:

> A pithy saying; a most useful aspiration, but absurd withal. For to make a fistful bigger than the fist, an armful larger than the arm, or to try and make your stride wider than your legs can stretch, are things monstrous and impossible. Nor may a man mount above himself or above humanity: for he can only see with his own eyes, grip with his own grasp. (ibid)

But, despite this catalogue of limitations, Montaigne returns to a possibility of transcendence, to the potential for transformation: humanity "will rise by abandoning and disavowing his own means, letting himself be raised and pulled up by purely heavenly ones." (ibid: 190) It is only by abandonment and letting-go of the attachment to dogma and false certainty that human beings can aspire to a "holy and miraculous metamorphosis". It is with these words that Montaigne ends the Apology.

How these words echo those of many mystics who would also argue that only through abandoning dogmatic belief, attachment and intention, and the certainty that accompanies them, can we open ourselves to the possibility of achieving a full realisation of the flux of being.

Samuel Beckett

Though it may seem surprising, Samuel Beckett can be considered as a successor to Montaigne – for Beckett is a deeply sceptical writer who strips away the cant, hypocrisy, false religiosity and unchallenged beliefs of formal Christianity and yet somehow keeps open a place for God or rather a place for wonder at the sheer fact of being here. There is a poignancy to Beckett's forensic interrogation of Christian ideas and practices, carried to such an extreme that there seems to be little left upon which he can depend or in which he can believe. But, against all the odds, he seems open to the idea that human beings exist in an improbable state of grace – given a life which, against all the odds, can be blessed with moments of joy or resigned equanimity.

In his 1958 play, *Krapp's Last Tape*, the protagonist sits in his cluttered room listening to old tapes of diary entries. He grumbles and curses, seemingly full of disgust at his pitiful observations and his fruitless attempts to make sense of his existence. Yet amidst this dismal catalogue of seeming failure he comes across a thirty-year-old recording of his description of a moment of bliss, lying in a punt on a river with his then lover: "We lay there without moving. But under us all moved, and moved us, gently, up and down, and from side to side. (Pause) Past midnight. Never knew such silence. The earth might be uninhabited." (McPherson 2006) Krapp tries to subject this brief recording to the same ridicule and invective he has heaped on every-thing else he has listened to, but there is something about it he can't dismiss and he returns to it. The play ends with him listening, trans-fixed, snared by a blissful episode he is unable either to understand or to deny.

Despite the fact that Beckett is often described and discussed as a misanthropic nihilist who seems to think the only redeeming feature of humanity is a gallows humour hurled in the face of pain and misery – despite this reading of his work, moments of quiet, peace and bliss crop up in surprising places throughout his plays and other writings – recounted with a warmth and almost-reverence that belies his misera-bilist reputation. Often the darkness is punctuated and relieved by a welcome light: "Bright at last close of a dark day the sun shines out at last and goes down". (Beckett 1995: 240)

There is a redemptive quality to Beckett's writing, a sense that by interrogating human existence, exposing the folly of becoming reliant upon idle assumptions, misguided beliefs and formulaic responses to the constant indeterminate twists and turns of lived experience –as if by facing up to and documenting such deluded thoughts and actions we can slough off the carapace of hubris and false optimism, finding instead a more humble sense of who we are and how we can live. Beckett seems to suggest a way of dealing with the contingency of life that involves first accepting that life is inevitably full of uncertainty, full of partings and uncontrollable events, and then accepting that it is only by acknowledging our inability to bring certainty to our lives through knowledge and control that we can learn to let go gracefully. The combination of courageous acceptance that all things pass, even those things we most wish to endure, and clarity of awareness of the folly of believing otherwise, can lead us to a state of equanimity – a state in which we suspend judgement and belief, and are less likely to be disturbed by attachment to false ideals and fantasies.

James Knowlson, in his biography, *Damned to Fame*, suggests that Beckett's distinctive approach to writing can be traced to his relation-ship with James Joyce and his discovery of a way to extricate himself from Joyce's influence. Beckett tells Knowlson: "I realized that Joyce had gone as far as one could in the direction of knowing more, [being] in control of one's material. He was always adding to it; you only have to look at his proofs to see that. I realized that my own way was in impoverishment, in lack of knowledge and in taking away, in subtracting rather than in adding". (see Anon 2010b) There are echoes here of the *apophatic* tradition in mystical literature – the way of unsaying and unknowing as a route to mystical equanimity. Beckett develops a way of writing that demonstrates in its methods a way of living, a way of attending to the flux and contingency of existence. By stripping away unnecessary ornament, narrative artifice and discursive formulae, he could find an equivalence for the realisation that a clear awareness of life's uncertainty, pain and evanescence can lead to moments of tranquillity, and to a tolerance and sympathy for those around us. Beckett sums up his realisation with characteristic brevity when he writes: "A story is not compulsory, just a life, that's the mistake I made, one of the mistakes, to have wanted a story for myself, whereas life alone is enough". (Melnyczuk 1996)

Samuel Johnson's approach to religion

In his magisterial biography of Samuel Johnson, Walter Jackson Bate, argues that Johnson's approach to religion is "empirical and analytic, and assumes that when one has cut off all illusions, what one has left is the truth". (Bate 1978: 283) Is there an echo here of Montaigne's God as what remains when man is "stripped of all human learning"?

Part IV

Buddhism and Daoism: sceptical mysticism

Buddha: "By becoming attached to names and forms,
not realising that they have no more basis
than the activities of the mind itself, error arises
and the way to emancipation is blocked".
(in Anon 2002b: 128)

Beauty and ugliness have one origin.
Name beauty, and ugliness is.
Recognising virtue recognises evil.

Is and *is not* produce one another.
The difficult is born in the easy,
Long is defined by short, the high by the low.
Laotzu.
(in Hamill and Seaton 2007: 22)

Introduction

While there are many Buddhists, perhaps a majority, who would dispute any idea of applying the term, "mysticism", to Buddhism, I am going to suggest that there are useful connections to be made between accounts of mystical states of consciousness and ideas in the literature of mysticism, and the accounts of states of mind (or no-mind) and ideas to be found in Buddhist writings and art. That there may be links between Buddhism and scepticism is an argument that is probably less contentious, indeed others have made this claim – for instance, Thomas McEvilley, in his book, *The Shape of Ancient Thought*, (2002) traces a probable historical interaction between Indian sages and ancient Greek philosophy, particularly in relation to the use of dialectical methods; while Nolan Pliny Jacobson makes a persuasive argument in relation to what he sees as a sceptical stance within Buddhism, particularly in relation to ideas about the self [see p. 131]; Stephen Batchelor has also argued that sceptical doubt and uncertainty are important aspects of Buddhist theory and practice (see Batchelor 1990)

Sunyata – "absence of self-existence" or "mutual dependency"

Before considering some of the parallels in practice and thought between Buddhism, scepticism and mysticism I'd like to focus on a key
term within Buddhist thought and practice, *sunyata,* or what I've
called the mutuality of existence. (Danvers 2006) Without some understanding of this term and its implications it is difficult to make
sense of other Buddhist ideas and practices. *Sunyata* also provides a
point of convergence between Buddhism, scepticism and mysticism as
will be seen as this chapter progresses.

The Sanskrit term, *sunyata,* is usually translated as "emptiness" or
"the void" but this can be very misleading, as it really refers to the
Buddhist insight that no entity (object or idea) exists in, or for, itself.
Existence consists of a web of mutually dependent or relational phenomena – none of which have any autonomous identity or self-
existence. They are *empty* or *void* of self-existence – what Adorno
may be implying by his term, "non-identity". [see p. 155]

The ideas surrounding *sunyata* are articulated in great depth in Nagar-
juna's *Sunyavada,* or "Doctrine of the Void", otherwise known as the
Madhyamika, the "middle way" – a way that, according to Watts,
"refutes all metaphysical propositions by demonstrating their relativity".(Watts 1989, p.62) Even the idea of *sunyata* itself, is relative and
'void'.

> It cannot be called void or not void,
> Or both or neither;
> But in order to point it out,
> It is called 'the Void.'
> (from the *Madhyamika Shastra,* in Watts 1989: 63)

This is reminiscent of Adorno's injunction not to consider "negative
dialectics" as a particular philosophical standpoint but as a method for
engaging with non-identity and the flux of dialectical play.

According to Murti, at one level the Madhyamika approach is a "critique of all philosophy". (1980: 123) He writes:

The essence of the Madhyamika attitude [...] consists in not allowing oneself to be entangled in views and theories, but just to observe the nature of things without standpoints. (ibid: 209)

This should not be interpreted as anti-intellectualism. Dreyfus provides a wonderful account of the rich culture of intellectual debate, analysis and critique within the Tibetan Buddhist monastic context. However the purpose of this individual and collective intellectual endeavour is to expose the contradictions and dualities inherent in *any* conceptual position or idea of self-existing identity.

Dreyfus describes the situation as follows:

[In relation to conventional truth] we distinguish a pot from other objects, such as a table, the maker of the pot, and the self who sees the pot. In discerning these conventional objects, we proceed through dichotomies such as self and other, agent and object, pot and nonpot, and the like. In this way we divide the universe of knowledge and reify these differences, as if these objects had their own essence and existed independently of each other. These dualities enable us to classify these objects and appropriate them, but they distort reality, for the objects do not in fact exist in the ways that we hold on to them. This distortion in turn leads to suffering created by our grasping at objects, which gives rise to attachment, aversion, and so on.

To free our minds, we need to undo the dualistic tendency to grasp objects by reifying differences. To succeed in this effort, we need to realize that things do not exist in the way we grasp them: that they are empty from existing through their own essence. (2003: 239-240)

Within Buddhism there are many different practices which are used to realise emptiness. These range from the intellectual dialectics of the Tibetan Madhyamika tradition, to the use of *koans* in Rinzai Zen, to *vipassana* meditation in the monastic traditions of south-east Asia, and to the practice of *zazen* or *shikan-taza* ("just sitting") in Soto Zen. These practices, and the discourses, disciplines and ethical codes that are integral to them, are used to release the participant from the bondage and misunderstanding that conventional, dualistic, objectifying thought engenders. Such practices are aimed at "depriving the mind of any object to hold onto," this "leads it to relinquish its habit of conceptualizing reality in dualistic terms". (Dreyfus 2003: 241)

As Dreyfus points out this should not be seen as a denial of the reality
of the material world or of our thoughts, beliefs and feelings.

> Because objects are beyond determination, they are not completely nonexistent.
> Hence, they can be said to exist provisionally or conventionally. Emptiness does
> not cancel out the conventional domain but relativizes it. (ibid: 241)

In other words, as objects only exist as discrete "objects" by convention (having no separate essential existence) they do have a conventional status or existence. Realizing *sunyata* or emptiness is to realise
that the conventions of dualistic thinking, interpretation and evalua-
tion *are* conventions. This holding in mind of two apparently contradictory states or perspectives is similar to the way in which we have to
deal with, on the one hand, our sensory experience of objects as material substances, and on the other hand, our knowledge through quantum physics of the indeterminate and insubstantial energies that make
up apparently substantial opaque objects. These distinctly different
views reflect two different levels of order, two different magnifica-
tions of observation and two different models or descriptions of what
is, in actuality, undifferentiated and irreducible.

Zen master Dogen and the mutuality of existence

Whether it is reasonable to consider the Japanese Zen master, Eihei
Dogen (1200-1253), as being a mystic is a debatable point about
which persuasive arguments can be made for and against. However, it
is possible to trace similarities of method, practice and ideas, between
Dogen and many of the sceptics and mystics we have been discussing.
I'd like to focus on a few areas of Dogen's thought in order to explore
some of these similarities.

In his writings, and he is one of the seminal writers in the history of
Japanese Buddhism, Dogen emphasises non-duality, the timelessness
inherent in each moment and the possibility that everyone can realise
enlightenment or Buddha-mind. Dogen makes use of paradox and
surprise in his writing as he tries to convey both the spirit and actuality of his insights into the relational field which is reality. For Dogen,
as with all Buddhist practitioners, the apparent separateness of entities

is an illusion, for all things are interdependent, manifestations of the mutuality of existence.

Dogen writes:

> An ancient Buddha said:
>
> The entire universe is the true human body.
> The entire universe is the gate of liberation.
> [...] The entire universe is the dharma body of the self.
> (in Tanahashi 1995: 163)

In a number of texts Dogen argues that to know the self is to lose the self and thus to find the self. The found self both is, and is not, the self that is lost. When the self is examined through bare attention, mindfulness or disinterested introspection, we realise that there is no essence or substantiality to the self. What we encounter are currents of sensation, feelings, thoughts and intentions, interwoven and in flux. There is no fixed core or unitary hub to this river of mental activity. Recognising that this is the case is to realise that "the entire universe is the gate of liberation", for there are no fixed limits or impermeable boundaries to the self. To experience the flux of sensations, moods and thoughts as events within the relational field of all that is, is to experience a transformed sense of self – to be liberated from a false understanding of what it is to be a person. It is as if a gate has opened to a new awareness of the self as an open fluid process rather than as a nucleic ego somehow separate from the world – a world outside or other. For Dogen, human beings are embodied minds participating in the relational field of the universe – thus the "entire universe is the gate of liberation". However, it is just as true to say that there can be no gate and no liberation because the universe is the self and the self is the universe.

Elsewhere Dogen writes: "An ancient Buddha said, 'The mountains, rivers, and earth are born at the same moment with each person". (ibid: 165) This is Dogen's way of expressing the idea of what Buddhists refer to as "dependent origination" or "mutual co-arising" – the mutuality of existence mentioned above. Dogen emphasises the interdependence of all phenomena, the interrelatedness of all that is. This doesn't mean that Dogen is suggesting that everything in the world is the product of human consciousness – that everything that exists is a mental or linguistic construct. He is careful to write that the universe arises "at the same moment with each person", that is, the universe and person are co-dependent, integral to each other. More precisely we might say that the "each" and "other" are indivisible and therefore they only have validity as terms within linguistic discourse, a discourse which divides in order to debate and discuss. So long as we recognise the conventions of division and compartmentalisation, and do not believe that these conventions are other than conventions, then Buddhists might say that no harm is done. But if we become attached to a belief that the divisions are actual, conditions of reality, we may find ourselves increasingly ill at ease with the world, alienated from what is.

Observation VIII – a question of give and take

As I am penetrated by the light of the world, so I reflect back light in turn. It is this give and take, flowing in and out, back and forth, that is the mutual respiration of all things. The world makes me, as I make it. Or perhaps, are we at either end of a seesaw that is always pivoting at our convergence?

Sitting and showing: Dogen and body-mind

At the centre of Dogen's teaching lies the practice of *zazen*, a form of sitting meditation also known in the Soto Zen tradition as *shikantaza*, just sitting. For Dogen, *zazen* is the primary Buddhist practice, an activity in which a person can learn how to be a Buddha, or to realise that they *are* a Buddha – manifesting Buddha-mind or Buddha-nature – yet doing this, as we'll see below, without striving or intending that this should happen.

In 1223, Dogen travelled to southern China with his teacher, Myozen, to visit the major Zen monasteries in the region and to learn what he could from the monks who were there. In 1221, when he was only twenty-one years old, Dogen had already received what is known as "dharma transmission" from Myozen, an acknowledgement that Dogen was considered to have mastered the teachings of Zen. However, Dogen was dissatisfied with his own understanding, or lack of it, and he thought that the teachers in Song dynasty China would enable him to realise his Buddha-nature.

During the first two years of his travels he seems to have been disappointed by the teachings he encountered, which were mostly devoted to *koan*-centred practices. [see p. 127] Then, in the summer of 1225, he went to the Tiantong Mountain monastery to meet the sixty-two year old abbot, Rujing. The meeting was one of the most important events in Dogen's life. He later wrote:

> I first offered incense and bowed formally to my late master, old Buddha Tiantong, in his abbot's room [...] He also saw me for the first time. Upon this occasion, he transmitted dharma, finger to finger, face to face (Tanahashi 1995: 5)

This seems to have been one of those moments when almost by being in each others' presence two people communicate at a very profound level. Rujing appears to have recognised that the time was ripe for a breakthrough in Dogen's practice and that he, Rujing, would do all he could to enable this to happen. He gave permission for Dogen to visit him at any hour for instruction and discussion, and Dogen made full use of this rare privilege.

According to Tanahashi, Rujing was an unusual teacher, who had little
time for the trappings of authority that went with his position. He never wore the ornately decorated robes that he was entitled to and argued
that what he taught was "the great way of all the Buddhas", something
that couldn't be confined within the label of "Zen School". (ibid: 6)
Rujing taught that to study Zen is to "drop away body and mind", that
is to let go of attachment to dualistic ideas and habits of thought, including notions of "body" and "mind". Rujing was undoubtedly a
forceful character. He ran a rigorous programme of instruction based
on the practice of *zhigan dazuo*, what we now know as *zazen*. As Rujing taught it, this was a practice which didn't involve the solving of
questions, as in the *koan*-based methods of most other Chinese
schools at the time. Rujing's sitting meditation was also not a practice
in which one sat *in order to become* enlightened. As Dogen was to
teach when he returned to Japan, *zazen* involves sitting just to sit, realizing Buddhahood in the very ordinary act of being attentive to one's
own existence – just being here.

In the year that they met, Rujing gave Dogen a certificate of transmission which states that he had achieved "direct penetration of merged
realisation" – the fullest tribute he could have received from his teacher. (ibid) Dogen continued to study at Tiantong Mountain even though
Myozen, his earlier teacher and companion, had died suddenly when
they first arrived at the monastery. Eventually Dogen said farewell to
Rujing and in 1227 he arrived back in Japan. One of the first things he
did on his return was to write his seminal essay, *Fukan Zazengi*, in
which he gives precise guidance on how to practice *zazen*.

Zazen, in Dogen's teachings, can be seen as having similarities to the
dialectical methods of the early Greek sceptics and the phenomenological enquiries of twentieth century philosophers such as Heidegger
and Merleau-Ponty. For Dogen, sitting in meditation involves a balancing act in which the sitter isn't attempting to prevent or eliminate
thoughts, feelings and phenomena that arise in consciousness, but
neither is the sitter adding to these thoughts and feelings – by commenting on them or prolonging them unnecessarily. Phenomena that
arise in the normal course of being conscious are observed or experienced without trying to repress them or hang on to them or spin further thoughts around them. By simply allowing them to arise and to

disappear without further action, reinforcement or what might be termed, meta-cognition, the sitter practices a form of phenomenological observation that seems close to what Edmund Husserl, Heidegger and Merleau-Ponty advocate. There may also be a link to Heidegger's use of the term *Gelassenheit*, "letting-be". [see p. 27] The sitter is letting-be or letting-go of the myriad phenomena that arise in consciousness from moment-to-moment, and in such a manner, exists or *is*, in as unadorned and pristine a fashion as possible. Being conscious, in this sense, is being open to the flow of phenomena, without interference or secondary action. This is sitting just to sit, being just to be.

When Dogen (in Kim 1987: 58) writes, "free yourself from all attachments, and bring to rest the ten thousand things", he points to the way in which becoming attached to particular things, ideas or feelings separates those things from the ever-changing relational field which is reality – a reality that is indeterminate and indivisible. Focusing on and attempting to grasp particular phenomena is to lose sight of the interrelatedness of *all* phenomena. To perceive phenomena as if they were isolated units rather than episodes in a continuum is for Dogen, and other Buddhists, to have a false understanding of how the world is. When we divide up the matrix of energies and potentialities (the phenomenal field) into bits, objects and things, we give rise "to the ten thousand things". In other words we lose sight of the wood for the trees – we lose sight of the undifferentiated field and believe that the universe consists of divisions, categories, separateness and bits – the "ten thousand things". Throughout his writings Dogen argues against false dichotomies and draws attention to the dangers of dualistic thinking in all its forms.

One key aspect of Dogen's teachings about *zazen*, is that when we sit and attend to what is going on within and around us, we can see clearly and precisely, with no secondary acts of discrimination and attachment clouding our perceptions. By attending to phenomena as they arise in consciousness, without attachment, we perceive the whole continuum and gain an insight into the harmony of the whole. The danger here is not that we *can* focus on aspects of the whole, for it is necessary that we discriminate between things in order to negotiate our way in the world and to communicate with each other, the danger is that we come to believe that the world is *actually* fragmented and compartmentalised – Dogen argues that to believe this is to be deluded and Buddhism is, above all, a path to awakening from delusion.

In another passage from the *Fukan Zazengi*, Dogen writes, "think of neither good nor evil and judge not right or wrong". (ibid) Here he advocates a course of action that is not unlike the injunction upon sceptics to suspend judgement, or to step sideways from the act of coming down on one side or the other of an argument or proposition. In a sense this teaching follows on from the previous one about becoming free of attachments. The Greek sceptics believed that as entities, including ideas and propositions, cannot be defined or precisely determined (*aoristia*, without boundary or limit) it is therefore ridiculous to act as if they can, by accepting one proposition or definition as if it was any more true or believable than any other. Dogen argues for a similar "suspension of judgement" (*epoché*, in sceptical terminology), and for similar reasons. If the universe as a whole is a manifestation of interdependence, mutuality and interrelatedness, then no part of it, be it a tree, a person or a proposition, exists independent of any other part. Thus *any* proposition (for instance, about good or evil) or judgement (about right or wrong) must always be to open to a contrary argument, and be uncertain, because propositions are always only partial and relative – they can never be absolute or complete.

Throughout the *Fukan Zazengi*, Dogen combines precise instruction with poetic suggestion to show how the practice of *zazen* enables a sitter to gain a clear view of the world in its dynamic relational glory by the simple, yet difficult, act of sitting, attending and being-here.
Dogen adds a further dimension to this practice by introducing the term, *hi-shiryō*, often translated as "non-thinking". According to Hee-Jin Kim, *hi-shiryō* refers to "a very special form of thinking beyond thinking and not-thinking". (ibid: 60) In this sense "non-thinking" is "objectless, subjectless, formless, goalless, purposeless". (ibid) Once again, this is a form of cognition that manifests the same kind of undifferentiated quality that perception has within *zazen* practice. Hence Dogen's paradoxical statement that, "the total experience of a single thing is the same as the total experience of all things" – for to see one thing clearly is to see it as integral to everything else. (ibid: 63)

The terms, "thinking" and "mind", have very particular meanings for Dogen – as they do within Buddhism as a whole. For Dogen, mind and body are inseparable, indeed the term, *shin-jin*, is often used by Dogen to refer to "body-mind" rather than mind on its own. According to Kim, "the human body, in Dogen's view, is not a hindrance to the realisation of enlightenment but the very vehicle through which enlightenment is realised". (ibid: 96) There is no hint here either of the dualistic polarising of body and mind, or the tendency of some Christian thinkers to marginalise the body or even to consider the body as something to be overcome or subjugated in order to become closer to God.

Not only does Dogen consider the body-mind to be an integrated whole, but he also recognises no essential separation between body-mind, *shin-jin*, and the world. Hence, Dogen's reference to the ancient Buddhist belief [see previous section] that, "the entire universe is the true human body. The entire universe is the gate of liberation". (Tanahashi 1995: 163) For Dogen, the world and body-mind are co-dependent and permeable. There is no fixed boundary between them. The body-mind is interwoven with the entire universe. The body-mind is a porous field of interpenetrating forces, a mingling of currents of being and awakening, a boundless site or clearing in which realisation can occur.

Observation IX – starlings

It is a cold grey January day. Under dreary clouds lies a field of stubble stippled with pale cut-off ends still sharp after months of frost and rain. Two huge oaks offer a filigree of branches to the sky. Suddenly, even in this gloomy wet light, a shadow curls across the ground. Up above a draught of darkness twists and flutters in a series of sinuous exclamations. A strange thrumming of wings marks the dance of thousands of starlings, choreographed to act as one, like flecks of waves chased by unseen breezes across a placid sea. Somehow each brain is tuned to its neighbours, countless bodies, connected by invisible elastic, eddy and ripple in fluid gestures of mutual delight. Is it one great being or many, thousands of intelligences or the shimmering thoughts of one playful imagination?

Awakening to living – mindfulness and self-construction

Buddhism can be seen as a body of ideas and practices aimed at enabling anyone to become fully awake – to become aware of what it is to
be here, to be alive at this moment every moment. In the Zen tradition
to sit in meditation is to treat all phenomena as being of equal importance, to be experienced and observed with equal care, acuity and
equanimity. There is no thought, sensation or feeling that is too mundane or too small to be unworthy of mindful attention. Awakening in
this context is to notice without commentary everything that arises, to
attend to the interwoven streams of sensations, narratives, images and
emotions that constitute consciousness. It is to notice that there are no
solid and fixed boundaries to our selves. Instead we notice that we are
a constantly changing hub of relationships with everything that surrounds us, humming with information-processing and imaginative
construction. We make ourselves from moment to moment, fashioning
ourselves out of the materials of our experiences.

Stephen Batchelor argues that the Buddha encourages us not to try to
destroy the self (which is how Buddhism is sometimes presented – as

a nihilistic religion) but to create the self, to fashion it out of the available material in the way that a carpenter creates something out of wood. The self is according to Batchelor (2010: 152) and the Buddha, "a project to be realised" rather than a transcendent entity with a fixed essence. The self we make in this way is a functioning responsive imaginative self that participates in the world and is inseparable from it. The Buddha's teachings are a recipe for action rather than a catalogue of dogmas or rules. He acts as a guide and navigator, helping anyone to enquire into the processes of living in order to re-orientate and revise who, and how, we are in the world. And a crucial starting point for this enquiry and re-visioning is the activity of sitting meditation, attending to the stream of sensations, thoughts and feelings that constitute the fluid materials of our self-making. In this sense we are an open work, a work in progress, never finished, never complete.

But, as the Buddha teaches, the way in which we attend to this flood of experiences is of crucial importance to our awakening. There is no point trying to distance ourselves or stand aside from the flow of sensations, thoughts and feelings, for this is both to remain asleep or unseeing and to attempt the impossible. As Batchelor writes, for the Buddha, freedom and equanimity is to be found "not by turning away from the world but by penetrating deep into its contingent heart". (ibid: 131) The art of attending in this way is to be fully present to the flow of experiences but not to add to it by commenting on it or trying to grasp at the flow, or by desiring it to be this way or that, or by responding to the flow with hope or fear. The crucial factor is to let it be, to let it flow, to be attuned to the rhythms and dynamics of movement, rather than trying to stop it – for it is unstoppable! To engage with life in this way is to experience how things are, how we are and to gain an understanding that enables us to let go of habits of thought, emotion and behaviour.

It is worth quoting Batchelor at length on the Buddha's awakening:

> [The Buddha] could remain fully present to the turbulent cascade of events without being tossed around by the desires and fears it evoked within him. A still calm lay at the heart of this vision, a strange dropping away of familiar habits, the absence, at least momentarily, of anxiety and turmoil. He had found a way of being in this world that was not conditioned by greed, hatred, or confusion. This was nirvana. (ibid)

And it is crucially important that the Buddha "found a way of being in *this* world", in the contingent reality of everyday experience. He came to terms with the complicated, messy, tangled web of everyday living. His particular insight and strategy was to realise that rejecting this reality in favour of a belief in an alternative reality was unhelpful, unnecessary and unwise. Liberation and equanimity does not lie in entering a state or place of transcendence, heavenliness or non-contingency. No, according to the Buddha, freedom and equilibrium are to be found in noticing what goes on here and now, by paying attention to the relational field of which we are an integral part.

This process of attending to what goes on inside, around and through us, with care and precision, includes attending to suffering in all its aspects (from mild dissatisfaction to severe pain and illness) – attending to the immediate felt pain and to the responses to that pain, the fear and anxiety that can exacerbate the pain itself. To pay attention to the whole spectrum of dissatisfaction, unease and dis-ease can have a profoundly calming effect on the restlessness and confusion we all feel from time to time, enabling us to experience a more peaceful equilibrium in the face of the difficulties of living. And paying attention to one's own unease and pain tends to lead to a deeper awareness of the suffering of other beings, which, in turn, gives rise to empathy and compassion, a sense of kinship and connectedness with all beings.

At the heart of the Buddha's teachings lies a belief that only by attending to one's own experiences in this world can we understand and begin to deal with the difficulties that we encounter. Daily experience, even at its most mundane, becomes the raw material out of which we remake ourselves and achieve a more balanced, peaceful and less fretful mode of being. Buddhism provides a box of tools for enquiring into *this* life – for finding out for ourselves, about who we are and how we are in the world. It also provides a variety of strategies for dealing with the constantly changing circumstances in which we find ourselves. One important factor in the processes of enquiring into, and dealing with, the contingencies of living is the recognition that uncertainty and doubt are unavoidable, indeed they are vital to any process of open-ended and continuous enquiry. There can be no final understanding or solution to the ever-changing conditions of living, no permanently valid answers to the constantly changing questions we pose.

Buddhism provides guidance on how we can find ways to live with uncertainty, to work our curious way through the puzzles and un-knowns we encounter from day to day. Buddhism, like scepticism, places doubting and unknowing at the centre of its teaching – as posi-tive qualities to be cultivated and valued.

Returning to Montaigne – on being awake

At this point I'm going to take a short detour to return to Michel de Montaigne in order to suggest a few similarities between Montaigne's attitudes to being and knowing and some of the Buddhist ideas and practices I have been discussing. In his writings, though typically not in any sustained or obviously schematic fashion, Montaigne has much to say about the importance of attending to what is happening from moment-to-moment. In the following remarks I am drawing upon Sarah Bakewell's excellent intellectual biography of Montaigne, *How to Live.* (Bakewell 2010)

Montaigne recognises how life slips away from him even as he per-ceives with great clarity its qualities, both joyful and painful. He writes, "I do not portray being. I portray passing. Not the passing from one age to another [...] but from day to day, from minute to minute". (ibid: 36) This heightened sense of mutability, of the evanescent na-ture of phenomena, imbues Montaigne's writings with poignancy and courage – the courage he demonstrates in facing the passing of each moment of life. Like the Buddha, Montaigne is a realist in his under-standing of the nature of lived experience. He accepts the finite uniqueness of each passing moment, realising with a kind of benign indifference that all he can do is to try to experience each moment as intensely as possible without clinging or hanging on to what can never be slowed or stopped.

At times Montaigne's observations are uncannily like the advice given by Zen teachers to their students. For instance he writes about walking alone in a beautiful orchard, noticing that his mind has a tendency to wander off, to dwell on "extraneous incidents". When this happens he brings his mind "back to the walk, to the orchard, to the sweetness of this solitude, and to me". (ibid: 38) This technique of watching the mind, noticing how and where it wanders, and gently bringing the attention back to what is going on now in the field of awareness is used extensively in Buddhism, as it is in many Christian approaches to contemplative prayer.

When Montaigne writes elsewhere, "when I dance, I dance; when I sleep, I sleep", (ibid) he seems to be almost quoting from the literature of Zen in which we find the following pithy remark by the Chinese Tang dynasty teacher, Yun-men (or Ummon in Japanese): "In walking, just walk. In sitting, just sit. Above all, don't wobble". (in Watts 1989: 135) Both authors suggest that we should try to avoid dividing our attention in such a way that we lose touch with what is going on at any particular moment, drifting in an inattentive way from object to object, thought to thought, feeling to feeling, without being aware of what we are doing. This is to be dreaming while only half awake, to sleepwalk through life. Montaigne, like the Buddha, suggests that life is too precious in its passing to be left unattended. As Seneca reminds us, "anyone who clears their vision and lives in full awareness of the world as it is [...] can never be bored with life". (Bakewell 2010: 111) Montaigne aspired to this state of awakening – a state, Buddhists believe, that was realised by the Buddha – whose name means "the awakened one" or the "enlightened one".

No matter

> no matter where
> we look surprises turn
> assumptions to ash,
> smoke twisting into
> all the shapes we can't
> imagine
>
> over there, I can only
> guess at what the journey
> brings:
> watermeadows
> strapped with iris-blades,
> meadowsweet sloughing
> cream skins in shadows
> where oaks lose their fisted
> roots

nothing is as we
expect it. Always
our expectations flit
like bats in and
out of what is and
what is not

existence is silent

true existence has no memory, has
nothing to say, nothing to describe.
it is. tathata. existence bears the
indelible mark of silence; it is
branded incommunicado.

it is branded incommunicado

Dogen and language as action

Like many Zen teachers, Dogen considers language as a form of action – a mode of doing and showing, as well as a mode of thinking and being. He employs language as a vehicle through which understanding can be demonstrated and realised. He often uses the word *dōtoku*, which is derived from the terms, *dō,* meaning "the way" and "to say", and *toku,* "to attain" and "to be able". (see Kim 1987: 79) *Dōtoku,* is not synonymous with language or words, it can also refer to silence as a form of expression. Dogen writes, "the wordless is not the same as expressionless [...] expression is not identical with utterance in words" (ibid), Kim argues that,

> *dōtoku* signifies both actuality and [the] possibility of expression — in other words, expression and expressibility. What is expressed intimates what is yet to be expressed — it is the Way. It also implies the understanding and grasping of the Way by expression. Furthermore, it expresses not what humans express so much as what the Way expresses". (Kim 2010)

For Dogen there are countless ways in which we can realise our Buddha-nature and countless modes of expression and communication through which we can manifest Buddha-mind – these range from verbal teachings and stories to the way in which we do things (for instance, walking, sitting, cooking), even the way in which we move or stand in a room. Indeed, Dogen shares with Jacob Boehme, a belief that the world and everything in it is a manifestation of cosmic creativity, an expression of what Dogen calls Buddha-mind or Buddha-nature, and Boehme calls God or *Ungrund*. As Kim suggests,

> all the phenomena of the universe – audible and inaudible, tangible and intangible, conscious and unconscious – are the self-expressions (*jidōshu*) of Buddha-nature and absolute emptiness. Nothing is excluded from this. (ibid: 80)

But we need to keep in mind that "absolute emptiness" here, refers to *sunyata*, which means "empty of self-existence" not empty in a spatial sense. That is, all things arise together and are interdependent – the mutuality of existence.

The use of *koans*

Koans, like Hakuin's, "What is the sound of one hand clapping?" or Hui-Neng's, "What is your original face?" are now the stuff of clichéd commentary or comedy, but within the Japanese Zen tradition, particularly the Rinzai school, they have a crucial role to play in a radical dialectical method that forces Zen students to experience the absurdities and paradoxes that arise within the web of language and intellectual speculation. The *koan* is used to pull the linguistic conceptualising rug from under our feet, to flip us over into suddenly experiencing the undifferentiated, ineffable mutuality of existence. In a kind of philosophical or existential slapstick the Zen teacher uses the *koan* to bring the student face-to-face with a reality-consciousness that is non-linguistic, immediate and wholly indeterminate.

Koan study, developed over many centuries by Chinese and Japanese teachers, can be considered as a dialectical method in the sense that the teacher presents a *koan* to the student, who experiences profound uncertainty and doubt as to how to respond to the *koan*. After what may be many attempts, the student formulates a response to the *koan* which seems to resolve the uncertainty through sudden insight (a state of mind, referred to as, *kensho*). The teacher determines whether the student's response demonstrates sufficient depth of realisation, and if so, provides another *koan* for the student to study. Study, in this context, may consist of reading the Zen literature on *koans*, for instance the *Zenrin Kushu* [see below] and, more importantly, bringing the *koan* into focus at the centre of the student's meditation practice. The student lives and breathes the *koan*, and it becomes the grain of irritating and subversive sand around which a pearl of understanding forms.

In the *Zenrin Kushu*, a collection of Zen poems and aphorisms, the paradoxical nature of this situation is evoked as follows:

> You cannot get it by taking thought;
> You cannot seek it by not taking thought.
> (in Watts 1989: 136)

Accounts of Zen students experiencing sudden insight or release (*satori* or *kensho*), often at moments when they're no longer able to grasp for the *right* (or *wrong*) response to the *koan*, echo descriptions of the sceptical state of *ataraxia,* which also often seems to arise when the sceptic lets go of the desire for *answers.* Julia Annas writes:

> [*ataraxia* or peace of mind, in sceptical terms, only arises] by not looking for it, merely being there when it arrives; and it arrives as a result of the rigorous investigation that makes it impossible to commit yourself for or against any position.(Annas 2000: 70)

There is no *right* answer to the *koan,* indeed there is no answer at all, in the usual sense. The student has to find a way around, or through, the dualistic thinking involved in making judgements or formulating logical answers. It is only when the student suspends belief and judgement, letting-go of the desire for answers, that they can then leap, or fall, into the state of openness, freedom and dynamic equilibrium which is *kensho.*

Writing about *koans* is notoriously difficult, for one reason because they are used within a very specific context: as part of the highly formalised private meetings between teacher and student known as *sanzen.* During *sanzen,* which may take place once or twice a day, the student demonstrates to the teacher his or her understanding of the particular *koan* upon which they are working. The key factor here is that the student has to *demonstrate* insight, rather than to explain what the *koan* means or to provide an answer to what might seem to be a question or riddle contained within the *koan.* This act of demonstrating insight, which is also demonstrating Buddha-mind in action, may be manifested in words or some other form.

The written records of these interactions suggest a very dynamic, often seemingly confrontational, relationship between student and teacher. Historically, the records provide an important resource for use by teachers and students: a source of *koans* for the teacher and a case study for the student. The most famous of these public records or cases in the Japanese Rinzai tradition are: the *Mumonkan* or The Gateless Gate; the *Hekiganroku* or Blue Cliff Record; and the *Shoyoroku* or Book of Serenity.

Hakuin's dialectics of doubt

The practice of *koan* study was developed within the Chinese Zen (known as Ch'an) tradition – indeed the Japanese term, *koan*, comes from the Chinese term, *kung-an*, meaning "public record". The most influential Japanese teacher to use the *koan* method was Hakuin (1689-1769), who revitilised the Rinzai school in the eighteenth century. In his short text, The Four Ways of Knowing of an Awakened Person, (see Low 2006: 29-39) Hakuin emphasises the importance of doubting as an integral part of *koan* study. Without "great will, great faith, and great determination" (ibid: 31) the student can make no progress. Without a powerful intent to work hard, to grapple with each *koan*, the student gets nowhere. Hakuin sees this as a remorseless enquiry, a drive to answer the question: "what is it that sees everything here and now. What hears?" (ibid) In other words *who* is it that enquires? Who is it that wants to know? Who is the "I" who needs to know? This burning necessity to question everything gradually turns into "a single mass of doubt, [the mind becomes] distressed, like a bird in a cage, like a rat that has gone into a bamboo tube and cannot escape." (ibid)

Hakuin urges his students to take nothing for granted, each time they think they have reached some understanding and clarity, which he refers to as "entering a crystal world", (ibid: 32) they mustn't stop to enjoy it. For, he points out, to think the state of mind they have reached is "wonderful and extraordinary" is to sink into attachment and delusion – to "fall into the cave of demons". (ibid) If they rest on their laurels and hold on to a sense of achievement they "will never see the real, awakened nature". (ibid) That is, they will never awaken to who they really are, never realise their Buddha-nature.

Hakuin's advice to go beyond an attachment to what might be seen as the fruits of doubt, can be considered as echoing the attitude of the early Greek sceptics who argue that only by suspending belief and judgement can true equanimity be realised. There may also be parallels with the mystical path of negation or *apophasis*, in which the mystic strips away all that might appear to be the positive signs of God and Godliness, in order to discover and realise that God, (or the *ungrund, in Boehme's terms*) is what is left when there is nothing more to be stripped away. The term "God" here, may be interpreted as referring to the phenomenal field – the mutuality of existence.

There are a number of different kinds of *koan*, which are used to guide the student through different aspects of Buddhist thinking and states of consciousness. *Gonsen koans* are particularly concerned with language – *gonsen* means literally "the study and investigation of words". (Miura & Sasaki 1965: 52) These *koans* are used by the teacher to bring the student to an understanding of how language can be used as a mode of liberation from its own limitations and constraints. Zen teaching is often summed-up in a four-line verse by Bodhidharma, the legendary figure who is reputed to have brought Buddhism from India to China in the early fifth century:

> Transmission outside doctrine,
> No dependence on words,
> Pointing directly at the mind,
> Thus seeing oneself truly, attaining Buddhahood.
> (in Stryk & Ikemoto 1965: xxvi)

Although there are a number of different ways of translating this quatrain, the basic elements of the teaching centre on the direct transmission of understanding or state of mind from person to person. Hakuin undoubtedly subscribes to this belief and method. He emphasises the active nature of Zen study and he uses verbal language, (as he uses visual expression – he is an accomplished and influential painter), as a powerful tool with which to free his students from attachment to habitual patterns of thought, feeling and belief.

For Hakuin, as for Dogen, verbal language is important insofar as it can be *used* as a means of release and realisation. Both teachers use language in unusual ways, often poetic in Dogen's case, often in a very physical, almost aggressive way, in the case of Hakuin. Both try to subvert expectations and raise questions about language itself and its effects upon thought and belief. The Zen master, Ummon, once said, "men of immeasurable greatness are tossed about in the ebb and flow of words". (in Miura & Sasaki 1965: 53) Dogen and Hakuin, in very different ways, try to bring their students to a realisation that we can avoid being tossed about by words, disentangling ourselves from the sticky web of language – finding instead a way to enlightenment *through* words, silences, gestures and pictures.

Buddhism – a sceptical analysis of self

In his book, *Buddhism: The Religion of Analysis*, (1970) Nolan Pliny Jacobson, argues that Buddhism is in many ways a sustained critique of western (Cartesian) notions of the self. His approach also raises some interesting points of similarity between Buddhist ideas and methods, and those of scepticism – both early Greek and more recent manifestations. I'd like to consider a few aspects of Jacobson's thinking about the self and some of the implications of these ideas in relation to mind and psychology.

Since Jacobson's book was published in 1970 there has been a considerable change in some areas of psychology and psychotherapy, not least in the development of methods and approaches that take account of Buddhist perspectives on the self and how Buddhist practices can be integrated into western therapies. Jack Kornfield, Maura Sills, John Kabat-Zinn, and others, have developed therapeutic approaches that involve a revision of ideas and beliefs about the self – addressing in different ways issues raised by Jacobson in his radical investigation into the psyche.

To give a flavour of Jacobson's combative style and an immediate sense of his argument here he is:

> Buddhism is opposed to all of the self-concepts in modern psychology for this simple reason, that selfhood is a process that has no self-identical, unitary, persisting soul or substance to which a concept might conceivably refer. There is no objection in Buddhism to conceiving of the self as a vast organisation of experience, a system always subject to change with each new experience of life. (Jacobson 1970: 29)

For Jacobson, the primary significance of Buddha's teaching is his identification of the self as a problematic concept, around which false assumptions and beliefs have arisen. Therefore one of the main purposes of Buddhist practice is to highlight fallacious thinking about the self and to analyse such thinking in order to gain a clearer and more balanced understanding. As Jacobson puts it, "the Buddha seeks to liberate the individual from the grip of a self-system" through meditative analysis. (ibid) While Jacobson is generally critical of western psychology, particularly the Freudian tradition in its many variants, he does acknowledge a kinship between Buddhism and the ideas and methods of Harry Stack Sullivan, (b.1892-d.1949) who coined the term "Self System" to refer to the currents of personality traits that shape an individual. Sullivan's conception of the self as only being understandable in relation to the network of social relationships within which it operates, was a key factor in the development of interpersonal psychoanalysis.

Individuals who cling to a self that they believe to be the substance or essence of who they are, are clinging to an illusion. For when we examine the self (for instance, in *zazen* or other forms of meditation practice) we find no evidence of a persisting substance, instead we observe a flux of impressions, feelings, thoughts and sensations that make up the moment-by-moment continuum of consciousness. This leads Jacobson to argue that Buddhist practice involves, firstly, a recognition that the conventional view of the self as a substance (and it *is* a convention) is mistaken, and secondly, that clinging to such a mistaken view leads to dissatisfaction and frustration. As Jacobson (ibid: 30) points out, "most of the questions [people] ask about life revolve around a fictional self". There is no harm, and there may be much good, in fictional imaginings, but there *is* potential harm and little good, in believing the fiction is real or believing the illusion is how things actually are – such beliefs are delusions. And it is delusions of this kind that Buddhism exposes through analysis.

Jacobson makes reference to a key concept in Buddhism, denoted by a term that is much-used in Indian philosophy, *Anattā*: "The doctrine of *Anattā* holds that the self is as insubstantial as the illusion of a perfect circle created by a whirling torch". (ibid) The whirling torch, if it moves fast enough, looks like a complete circle, but the appearance is deceptive. Similarly when we watch a film we see people moving about, speaking and laughing and having adventures. For the duration of the film we are engrossed and we set aside (or forget) that we're watching a series of still images projected very rapidly on to the silver screen. But when the film stops we remember that it *is* a film and

think about it as we do other imaginative narratives. Buddhist meditation practice enables us to watch the flow of consciousness as we do a
film, but also, crucially, to see that the flow *is* a flow, a fluid process
that is ungraspable and unstoppable – not something to which we
should or can cling. Hanging on to the idea that the film is real and
substantial, or believing that what we see on the screen are actual people in the cinema with us, is to be deluded and sooner or later will lead
to disappointment and alienation.

In the Buddhist traditions, the self is considered as a process rather
than a "thing". *Anattā*, often translated as "no-self" or "not-self", refers to the absence of any permanent essence or substance. From this
perspective there is no point in clinging to a self that has no substance
or essence. If desire flows from a belief in this illusory source, it can
never be fulfilled. As Jacobson points out the Buddhist view is radically different to the western idea of the self or "soul" as the continuing kernel of a person's identity, the ego at the centre of our being.
Jacobson argues that the West has tended to institutionalise this idea
of the permanent essential self. The typical westerner projects his or
her craving for things, substances and permanency on to a world that
consists of impermanent and fluid energies. He or she objectifies and
reifies a sense of "I" and "you" and "it" in a way that leads to a belief
that this is the way the world is – but as we've seen, from the Buddhist
perspective, it isn't. Many ego-based psychological theories, and the
therapies emanating from them, can be seen as institutions that legiti-
mise misunderstandings about the nature of the world.

Jacobson argues that the Buddha's insights and teachings may help

> individuals to accept the basic indeterminacy of the human creature, the ambiguity
> and formlessness at the centre of their lives [against which they] try to fix their
> identity upon some cluster of transient identifications. (ibid: 61)

If we attach ourselves to what is evanescent, ever-changing and indeterminate it is no surprise that we often become unhappy and dissatisfied with our lot. As Jacobson points out, Buddhism provides a way of
re-orientating our beliefs and behaviour, away from this misguided
view of the way things are. It seeks to liberate us from compulsive
behaviour, *tanhā*, and ignorance or delusion, *avidyā*.

Agents of Uncertainty

Jacobson quotes, Shwe Zan Aung:

> Life in the Buddhist view of things is like an ever-changing river [...] receiving from the tributary streams of sense constant accretions to its flood, and ever dispensing to the world around it the thought-stuff it has gathered along the way. (ibid: 83)

Another view of Buddhist scepticism

Another perspective on the relationship between Buddhism and scepticism can be gleaned from the final volume of the journals of Thomas Merton, written while preparing for, and undertaking, his long-awaited trip to Asia in 1967-68. Merton quotes from T.V.R. Murti's book, *The Central Philosophy of Buddhism* (1980). Merton is particularly interested in passages in which Murti is explaining to his readers some of the key points of the Madhyamika school of Buddhism which, he argues, gives philosophical expression to the views of the historical Buddha. According to Murti the Buddha rejected dogmatism in all its forms. He was equally against both idealism and materialism. The Buddha had no interest in replacing a positive dogmatic statement with a negative one and he didn't propose a "third position lying between two extremes but a no-position that supersedes them both". (in Merton 1999: 253) This is the Buddha's "middle way".

This positionless position, is also taken by the Buddha in relation to the question, is there a self? Murti writes:

> Note that the Buddha neither said "there is a self" nor "there is not a self". But among many Buddhists there appears to be a kind of dogmatism that says "there is not a self" instead of taking the true middle". (ibid)

Murti points out that the Buddha's usual response to this question was to remain silent. The purpose of Buddhist dialectics, at least in the Madhyamika tradition, is to deliver "the human mind from all entanglements and passions. It is freedom itself". (ibid) Like the ancient Greek sceptics all assertions and theories are subjected to analysis and shown to be flawed, partial and conditional. The Buddhist and the sceptic realise the emptiness of all claims to certain or absolute truth, they realise instead how all views are relative and interdependent. In so doing they suspend definitive judgements and beliefs, continuing instead to explore and examine phenomena as they arise.

Thomas Merton comments on his readings of Murti's philosophical exposition, writing that the Madhyamika teachings shouldn't be interpreted as an escape from worldly affairs into the realms of an ideal or abstract transcendence. Instead, they should be seen as a guide to how to transform human consciousness "by a detached and compassionate acceptance of the empirical world in its interrelatedness. *To be part of this interrelatedness*". (ibid: 261) Again Merton argues that Madhyamika Buddhism doesn't propose a particular truth to supplant or counter any other "truth". Rather the Madhyamika dialectical method is used to reveal the absurdity of any truth or position, by carrying an argument in its own terms to the many, often very divergent, logical conclusions that arise from it – conclusions which the proponent of the argument can themselves accept. Merton comments in ironical Christian terms: "Is this sadism? No, it is compassion! It exorcises the devil of dogmatism". (ibid: 262) It is likely that Pyrrho, Sextus Empir-

icus and Montaigne would agree with him. Elsewhere in his last journals Merton quotes from the Ashtavakra Gita, part of the ancient Sanskrit canon of Vedanta (Hindu) literature: "Neither reject nor accept
anything". (ibid: 91) Pyrrho would probably be nodding and shaking
his head in sceptical fellowship!

Calculation, meditation and unknowing – Stephen Batchelor

In his book, *The Faith to Doubt: Glimpses of Buddhist Uncertainty*,
(1990) Stephen Batchelor provides some interesting insights into the
role of questioning and doubt in Buddhist practice. Although Batchelor makes no direct reference to the ancient Greek sceptics, his remarks can be seen as suggesting a link between the ideas and methods
of Buddhists and sceptics.

Batchelor contrasts two different kinds of questioning and thinking:
calculative and meditative. He draws upon Heidegger's use of these
terms to identify two very different approaches to thinking. On the one
hand, calculative thinking, is the mode of cognition we employ to
solve problems, to analyse situations and concepts, to work out what
we are going to do and how we are going to do it. This is a practical,
scientific and usually goal-orientated way of thinking – it is concerned
with executing our intentions, satisfying the desires and hopes of our
ego-centred self. On the other hand, meditative thinking is concerned
with understanding, reflecting, making sense in depth, realising what
things mean, exploring the true value of things.

Calculative thinking is important insofar as it enables us to get things
done, to construct theories and buildings, to make things happen. But,
if it becomes too dominant, if it is not counter-balanced by meditative
thinking, it becomes manipulative, overly-selfish and destructive.
Meditative thinking enables us to place our ideas and actions in a wider context, to question the value and meaning of our activities – particularly to see how what we do affects others and the world about us.
Meditative thinking is also connective thinking, opening up to the
implications of actions, ideas and events. While calculative thinking
leads to a sense of knowledge as something to be earned and the world
as a place in which we can exercise and satisfy our intentions and

needs, meditative thinking tends to consider knowing and the world as gifts or acts of grace.

Batchelor argues that meditative thinking accepts and celebrates the unknown, acknowledging that human knowledge is partial and conditional, that there are mysteries and zones of possibility that we can only sense by intuition and imagination – which cannot be calculated or analysed by reason alone. Although calculative thinking can be creative and inventive in its own terms, meditative thinking tends to be associated with a more playful creativity – "thinking outside the box", to use a popular and telling phrase.

While calculative thinking is concerned with questioning in relation to specific goals and analytical parameters, meditative thinking tends to be concerned with questioning what things mean and how things exist in relation to the whole. Indeed meditative questioning is often directed at the great puzzles of existence itself: what is it to *be*; what part do we play in the vast web of life; how do we relate to everything around us; how should we act in relation to ourselves, to other beings and to the world? Crucial to this kind of thinking is having a sense of proportion and value, and realising that we often need to sit with our own not knowing in order to understand or intuit at a deeper level. Batchelor suggests that unknowing is an important aspect of meditative thinking – unknowing in the sense of a positive act of letting-go of the desire to calculate, manipulate and analyse, and, in so doing, realising the interdependence of knower and known, the interaction between observer and observed. While calculative thinking involves the need to fulfil expectations, meditative thinking involves the letting-go of expectations, sitting without expectation or attachment to a goal. Calculative thinking tends to assert a sense of self that is built out of certain knowledge, reliable information and verifiable facts; meditative thinking affirms a sense of self that is porous and open, fluid and indeterminate.

It hardly needs pointing out that meditative thinking is particularly associated with the religious domain and with mysticism, but if we take up Batchelor's suggestion that mystery and unknowing are integral to meditative thinking, we can also make a connection with scepticism. The sceptic recognises the partiality and uncertainty involved in calculative thinking. There can be no certain knowledge and no certain truth. There are always equally valid counter-arguments to any position taken. There are always limits to what we know, and always mysteries to be explored – hence the sceptic's suspension of belief or judgement and the unending nature of sceptical enquiry, which can never come to conclusions.

We also need to keep in mind that *both* calculative and meditative modes of thinking are important. Exercised in a balanced way they enable us to develop the breadth of our human capacities. One potential danger of the dominance of calculative thinking is that it may lead us to consider other beings and the world as *things* which exist to serve our own purposes and to satisfy our individual or collective human needs. A potential danger of the dominance of meditative thinking is that it may lead to inaction and to an uncritical acceptance of the status quo, or to an equally selfish (and deluded) retreat from the world of human affairs and frailties. It is worth reminding ourselves that Buddhist practitioners like Dogen and Hakuin, Christian mystics like Hildegard of Bingen and Meister Eckhart, and sceptics like Montaigne and Hume, were exemplary thinkers in both modes – effective as administrators, organisers, critics and writers, as well as being very effective as teachers and agents of awakening.

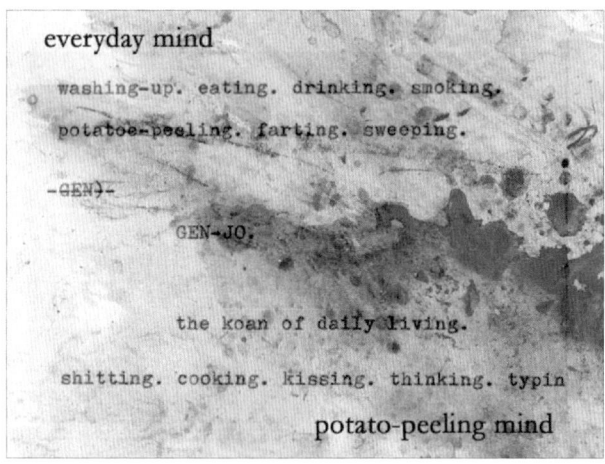

everyday mind

washing-up. eating. drinking. smoking. potatoe-peeling. farting. sweeping.

-GEN)-

GEN-JO.

the koan of daily living.

shitting. cooking. kissing. thinking. typin

potato-peeling mind

Zen and "everyday mind"

The Japanese Soto Zen master, Sekkei Harada, makes reference to the famous *koan* in which: "Joshu asked his master, Nansen, 'What is the Way?'" – that is, "what is the Way of the Buddha". Nansen replied, "Everyday mind is the Way". (Harada 1998: 60)

Harada suggests that: "The words 'everyday mind' express the condition of our lives free of our own ideas and opinions. Washing one's face, brushing one's teeth, talking, taking meals, working – all these activities [can] take place before thought". (ibid: 164) That is, before we weave our chattering mind around them – adding layers of commentary and feeling to the activities themselves. Everyday actions are an actualisation of Buddha Mind if we don't cling to them or add unnecessary layers of hopes, intentions, worries and expectations to them.

The highest we can aspire to is the ordinary, the everyday, the humdrum – the art, or creative practice, of living. Attending, without clinging, to the stream of everyday experiences is a profound creative activity. But, as Sawaki Roshi points out: "Everyday life has rainy days, windy days, and stormy days. So you can't always be happy. It's the same with *zazen*". (Uchiyama 1990: 52) Uchiyama adds that *zazen* is at heart "the practice of continuous awareness in the midst of delusion, without attachment to delusion or enlightenment". (ibid) In a similar vein Georges Dreyfus suggests, the everyday sound of *two* hands clapping may, in the end, be more important than the rare sound of *one* hand clapping. (Dreyfus 2003)

Speaking very much in the tradition of Dogen and Bankei, Sawaki Roshi de-mythologizes and debunks the notion that *satori* or enlightenment are extraordinary or special attainments. At one point he goes so far as to say: "there is no way to fail in becoming a Buddha [.....] The night train carries you along even when you are sleeping". (Uchiyama 1990: 54) He suggests that however we may clothe *satori* or enlightenment or Buddha Mind in special properties, there is in actuality nothing special about realising Buddha-nature – it is to be just as we are, no less and no more. The view of Buddha Mind as special is delusive in that it depends on attachment to the idea of specialness, it is to sit in meditation *in order to become* special (enlightened). It is to sit, polishing the tile of the self in the hope that it will become a mirror of enlightenment – but, as Nangaku [in Chinese, Nan-yüeh] (see Watts 1989: 96-97) and Dogen [in the *Fukanzazengi*] argue, it never does. Paradoxically, as Dogen points out, if we polish the tile *for its own sake*, with no thought of reward, we may well realise Buddha Mind. (see Harmless 2008: 208)

Watching the fishes in the stream

One of the many difficulties of the apparently simple act of *zazen*, is to be aware of the endless stream of perceptions, thoughts and feelings, without becoming attached to any one of them – attending to the stream but not grasping at the fishes in it. This is reminiscent of the methods of ancient Greek sceptics who argued that we should not become entangled in the divisive web of language which tends to pin down or define what is intangible and indefinable. The sceptics thought that as nothing could be said to have a fixed, independent or absolute existence, including human ideas and opinions, it was best to suspend judgement and belief, and not to become attached to either side of an argument. Similarly we could describe *zazen* as sitting in non-attached attention, being aware of the endless creative play of opposites and possibilities, without taking sides.

The German-born Theravada Buddhist monk, Nyanaponika Thera, described the state of mind that is exercised in this kind of sitting meditation as the "clear and single-minded awareness of what actually happens *to* us and *in* us, at the successive moments of perception". (in Epstein 2004: 31) This mode of awareness is also often referred to as "bare attention". The Buddhist psychiatrist, Mark Epstein, traces parallels between bare attention and the advice Sigmund Freud used to give to trainee psychoanalysts in conducting sessions with patients (it also seems to connect with the methods of the ancient Greek sceptics). Freud writes that the psychoanalyst should "suspend [...] judgement and give impartial attention to everything there is to observe". (ibid: 32) According to Epstein, Freud describes an "optimal state of mind" that has two important qualities: on the one hand, "the absence of reason or deliberate attempts to select, concentrate, or understand"; and on the other, an "even, equal, and impartial attention to all that occurs in the field of awareness". (ibid) This sounds remarkably similar to the state of mind of the *zazen* practitioner, of many mystics practicing contemplative prayer, and of a Pyrrhonist sceptic trying to achieve and maintain a state of equanimity. Note also that the aspiration is to attend to *this* world, to the everyday reality that presents itself moment-by-moment to the embodied mind, not to seek other-worldly experiences or to escape into states of mind that befuddle the senses or that seem to offer us an alternative reality to that in which we find ourselves in our daily lives. The emphasis is on *being here* not on being, or imagining being, somewhere else.

Daoism, impermanence, process and relativity

NB. *There are a number of different ways of denoting Daoist terms in English – depending on the form of Romanisation that is used: Tao or Dao; Lao tzu or Laozi; Daodejing or Tao te ching; Chuang-tzu or Zhuangzi; and so on. I will use Dao, Laotzu, Daodejing and Chuang-tzu – as I have grown accustomed to employing these commonly used terms. Controversy and uncertainty surround the authorship and dates of composition of the two seminal texts of Daoism – the Chuang-tzu and the Daodejing. It seems likely that the latter was written first, probably by many authors. Both texts seem to have been in use by the third century B.C.E. In 1993 fragments of the Daodejing were found written on bamboo slips, preliminary tests suggest a date of around 300 B.C.E. (Littlejohn 2005)*

Some of the Buddhist perspectives discussed above can be related to aspects of Daoist philosophy and practice. Both traditions share a belief in impermanence, change and process as characteristic features of the universe. They both also place emphasis on non-attachment and tolerance, and on non-discriminating attention, as appropriate ways of responding to change and impermanence. In this section I'm going to focus on one aspect of Daoism: that is, a belief in the wisdom of achieving a state of balance in opinion, perception and state of mind – a belief that echoes the ideas and practices of Madhyamika Buddhism and scepticism and, I suggest, a belief that can be related to the notion of the *contrarium* as described in Part V.

In a fascinating analysis of Daoist philosophy, Hans-Georg Moeller (2006) writes about the distinctive Daoist approach to ethical issues and to the clash of competing ideas and viewpoints. Moeller (ibid: 99) makes reference to an ancient Chinese tale about an old man living at a frontier fort whose horse runs away. His neighbours are sad and full of sympathy for his loss, but the old man seems to be unconcerned and asks them how they can be sure that it is bad luck. Months later the horse returns, bringing with it other horses of fine quality. The old man's neighbours are delighted and congratulate him. He seems un-moved and this time he asks them how they can be sure it is good luck. The horses enable the old man to become prosperous. His family share in his seeming good fortune until one day his son breaks a leg while out riding. His neighbours are very distressed by this turn of events but the old man is once again unperturbed and asks them how they know that this is bad luck. Not long afterwards enemy tribesmen attack the fort and many young men are killed. However, as the son has a broken leg he cannot fight and both the old man and his son are unharmed.

The Daoist interpretation of this story is that we can never know when good luck will become bad, or when bad luck will turn into good, and therefore the old man is wise in not getting too carried away by the turn of events. He remains in a state of equanimity – neither particu-larly happy, nor overly despondent. The old man recognises that as we live in a stream of ever-changing sensations, experiences and events, each inextricably linked to what comes before and to what follows, we can never be sure of what is good or bad. The fact that life is a contin-uum means we can never be certain how to separate one moment or event from another. All such separations or divisions can only be highly provisional and temporary. Even the old man's neighbour's can see that what happens can be both good *and* bad, positive *and* nega-tive. But because they cling to the idea that things are either good *or* bad they are upset by change, while the old man accepts change and is not too disturbed.

Not only is the old man not disturbed by changing events he maintains that he doesn't know whether they are good or bad. He remains unmoved by different interpretations and doesn't attach himself to any particular truth claim – as Moeller writes: "The sage is the only one who does not take sides". (ibid: 107) Because the old man doesn't know whether something is good or bad he doesn't become emotionally involved on one side or the other. He remains open to both possibilities. In a sense he is like the sceptic who suspends belief and judgement because he is still enquiring, still investigating – he doesn't believe he has found an answer.

Although the old man is as subject to the vicissitudes of life as his neighbours he doesn't suffer the added pain of having a belief in good fortune battered out of him and turned into an opposite belief in bad luck. He avoids the emotional upheavals and storms that afflict his neighbours. Sad as he may be when his horse runs away or when his son breaks a leg, his suffering is not made worse by emotional attachment to a false understanding of what these events mean. Likewise, he is no doubt pleased to see his horse return with others and to see his son unharmed by his enemies, but his pleasure is not exaggerated by believing that this is evidence of good luck. To him there is no substance or definitive truth in the idea that he has been favoured with good luck or cursed with bad luck and he thus avoids the worst extremes of emotion that seem to upset and confuse his neighbours.

The need for impartiality and non-attachment to either side of an argument or assertion is a recurring theme of the Daodejing (Tao te ching). In Chapter 49 this impartiality is articulated in what may seem a paradoxical, or even nonsensical, statement about the moral outlook of a Daoist sage:

> That which is good
>   he holds to be good.
> That which is not good
>   he also holds to be good.
> Thus he attains goodness.
>
> That which is true
>   he holds to be true.
> That which is not true
>   he also holds to be true.

Thus he attains truth.
(ibid: 106 translated by Moeller)

Moeller points out that this amoral moral teaching needs to be seen in the context of a philosophical idea articulated throughout the Daodejing, that is, that all assertions, ideas and claims are subject to change and possible reversal – they are always relative and provisional. There is no permanence anywhere, either in nature or in the realm of human values and knowledge. There can be no absolute judgements or definitive points of view, because nothing has a fixed essence or substance. This process-based outlook, which seems to anticipate understandings in contemporary physics – hence the success of Fritjof Capra's *The Tao of Physics* (2000) – can be very unsettling to those who seek absolute knowledge upon which to build certainty of belief. Connections can also be made with the process philosophy of John Dewey. [see p. 31]

Toshihiko Izutsu, in his study of the *Chuang-tzu*, (1984) sheds light on Daoist ideas about process, relativity and the absence of essences. He suggests that Daoism undoubtedly espouses a form of relativism, but it is

> a peculiar kind of relativism based on a very peculiar kind of mystical intuition: a mystical intuition of the Unity and Multiplicity of existence. It is a philosophy of 'undifferentiation' which is a natural product of a metaphysical experience of Reality, an experience in which Reality is witnessed as it unfolds and diversifies itself into myriads of things and then goes back again to the original Unity. (ibid: 319-320)

We can recognise affinities with other accounts in mystical literature of the unity of all things and of the Many in the One, the One in the Many. [see Spinoza, p. 58 above] The distinctive feature of the Daoist view is the emphasis on change and process – the cycle of differentiation and undifferentiation, unity and multiplicity, which is always at work throughout the universe. Things arise out of the undifferentiated field of possibilities, only to return to the field. There is no permanent division or separation between things, only a temporary state of apparent distinction.

Izutsu argues that a Daoist practitioner experiences the world, or aspires to, in its undifferentiated state, a state in which "all ontological distinctions between things become dim, obscure, and confused, if not completely destroyed. The distinctions are certainly still there, but they are no longer significant, essential". (ibid: 319) Distinctions are subject to change and revision, they are not permanent or absolute. This is markedly different to the view of the other major tradition of philosophical thought in China, Confucianism. For the Confucian, "everything is marked off from others by its own 'essence'". (ibid: 321) These essential differences are permanent and are the basis for the ways in which we categorise phenomena and organise society. Hierarchies of rank and status are built upon such essential distinctions, and social order is maintained by carefully upholding such differences. The Daoist has a very different view. He or she "sees the world as a vast and limitless space where things merge into one another". (ibid) The Daoist universe is a multi-dimensional field of fluid energies and potentialities rather than of clearly defined *things*. All distinctions between things are temporary and all apparent things are interrelated. The universe is a vast web of relationship and intermingling, in which apparent differences are relative.

This distinctive understanding of how the universe is composed is echoed in a similarly distinctive view of the mind. Seen from a Daoist perspective there are two primary states of mind, in Izutsu's words: "galloping around" or "sitting still and void". (ibid: 324) The term, *hsin*, refers to the state of mind in which our thoughts flit about, chasing phenomena or ideas, fretting about this and that, running after one idea of truth or another, changing opinions and positions. This is the state of mind of the old man's neighbours in the above story. In the other state the mind seems to be at ease, letting-go, open to the flow of phenomena and events, accepting the impermanent nature of reality – the state of mind of the old man. The former is characterised by clinging to, or being lead around by, distinctions and differentiations; the other is being attuned to, and at rest in, the undifferentiated field of energies and potentialities. This latter state is denoted by the term, *wu-hsin*, often translated as "no-mind", (Watts 1989: 23) or in Buddhist terms, Buddha-mind.

The Daoist idea of relativity extends beyond the world of phenomena and objects to the domain of concepts and judgements, for "our judgement is bound to be relative, one-sided, ambiguous, and unrelia-

ble, for the object of the judgement is itself ontologically relative".
(ibid: 323) *Things* are impermanent and ever-changing, so it's no surprise that our judgements can never be fixed or absolute. In the
Chuang-tzu it is argued that heated debates, in which opponents claim
that this is right or that is wrong, are futile because the objects of debate and reality itself are ever-changing and indefinite. There is no
stable, permanent reality, made up of things with fixed essences, about
which we can be objective or about which we can form absolute distinctions or judgements. Things only exist in relation to other things in
a fluid and ever-changing relational universe. Thus the Daoist sage,
like the ancient Greek sceptic, suspends judgement and maintains a
state of equanimity.

Observation X – throwing stones in the pool

From the creased pages of an old paperback, Epictetus whispers: "Men are disturbed not by the things which happen, but by opinions about the things which happen". He has a point. So often we add to the pain of an event by piling on top of it a heap of opinions and reflections and speculations, until the event itself has been buried. The pain is perpetuated not by the event but by the heap that obscures it. Get rid of the heap and the pain will be proportionate to the event. But it is hard to take Epictetus' advice, no matter how much we agree with it. It is even harder to follow another of his suggestions: "It is the act of an ill-instructed man to blame others for his own bad condition; it is the act of one who has begun to learn, to lay the blame on himself; and it is the act of one whose learning is deep, neither to blame another nor himself".

I look up and the sky is full of interesting pools and rivers, islands and beaches, wavy patches of grey and streaks of pink, arrows of white and faint eddies of silver. Only the faintest of edges marks the horizon. The sea shimmers and chatters in thousands of voices, pulsating with countless moods and thoughts. As I gaze into the distance another observation of Epictetus comes to mind: "If a man says to you that someone has been speaking ill of you, don't disagree with what has been said. Instead reply that the man could have known only a few of my faults. Invite him to meet me and I will tell him of the many faults he has missed".

Interweaving: scepticism, mysticism and equanimity

To end this chapter I'd like to look again at possible similarities in some of the aims or consequences of scepticism, Buddhism, Daoism and Christian mysticism. In its ancient Greek context scepticism offered practical guidance in how to cultivate equanimity and peace of mind in the face of life's difficulties and upsets. In this regard the aim of sceptics like Pyrrho was similar to that of the Epicureans and Stoics, who also offered methods for developing inner harmony. It was the methods and philosophical ideas of the sceptics that differentiated them from their peers.

Terence Penelhum (1983: 289) reminds us that sceptical practices were intended to lead to a state of equanimity and freedom from the "confusion and anxiety" brought on by the "competition between contending dogmas". By avoiding dogmatic adherence to either side in an argument, by suspending judgement and belief, an attitude of continuous enquiry and openness to all possibilities could be developed and maintained. Sceptical equanimity was dynamic rather than passive or quietist – suppleness, fluidity and curiosity typify the sceptical mind. Tolerance and acknowledgement of diversity and difference seem to follow from the skilful use of sceptical methods – an alternative to rigid adherence to dogmatic beliefs and values.

In a similar way Daoist practitioners aim at developing a state of mind that is at ease with the ever-changing flow of events, a state of inner harmony and freedom from becoming entangled in the web of relations and interactions that constitutes the world of human affairs. Buddhist teachers also provide guidance on how to develop equanimity of mind in relation to the trials and tribulations of life – how to become free of attachment to feelings, ideas and things that are inevitably going to change and pass away. Christian mystics also advocate ways of dealing with the pain and dissatisfaction that arises when we cling to the "things of the world", our dissatisfaction rooted in a feeling that we are separate from the rest of creation. By re-orientating our sense of identity and selfhood in relation to God – the infinite flux and mutuality of existence – we can experience peace and fulfilment.

NB. Readers interested in the history of possible interactions between ancient Greek thought, particularly scepticism, and Indian philosophy, particularly Madhyamika Buddhism, are encouraged to read Thomas McEvilley's excellent study of these matters, The Shape of Ancient Thought: Comparative Studies in Greek and Indian Philosophies (2002. 454-505) and my brief commentary in Picturing Mind. (Danvers 2006: 89-94)

Part V

The *contrarium*: a dialectical seesaw

"If you love something, you love nothing.
God is neither this nor that..."
Angelus Silesius
(in Barthes 2005: 60)

"I don't know what to do
two states of mind in me"
Sappho, fragment 51
(in Carson 2003: 107)

"It is the opposite which is good for us".
(Heraclitus, in Burnet 1971: fragment 46)

Introduction – the *contrarium*

At the end of my book, *Picturing Mind* (Danvers 2006) I made use of
the term, *contrarium*. I'd like to do so again, in order to develop ideas
about dialectics and to suggest ways in which the overwhelmingly
dualistic nature of western thought can be countered or subverted. I
first came across the term in an essay by the American poet, Robin
Blaser. (1974:35-62) Blaser mentions it within a discussion of the
metaphysics of light tradition in Christian theology. He refers to the
contrarium again in his book on his friend and fellow-poet, Jack Spicer, but again, it is mentioned only in passing. (Blaser 1975: 278) The
image and idea of the *contrarium* seems particularly useful as a way
of dealing with the articulation of doubleness and the balancing of
polarities.

We live in a world of hard and soft *things*, handling objects that have
weight, texture and substance. Yet, at the same time, we perceive these things as shifting patterns of light, colour and tone, forms that
change and reform themselves as we interact with them, eventually
becoming other entities as they are dis-integrated or subjected to processes of growth or decay. We also know, through the extended sen-

suality of our sciences, that these apparent substances are also fields of energy in constant motion, devoid of any solid essence. One way or another we have to develop a dynamic equilibrium at the point at which these opposing understandings collide. We have to live in the continuum that is also a dis-continuum, manifesting a certainty that is also a profound uncertainty. This is one of the most difficult aspects of contemporary living.

As William Empson, the author of *Seven Kinds of Ambiguity*, points out: "life involves maintaining oneself between contradictions that can't be solved by analysis". (in Phillips 2005) This state of juggling or balancing equally valid yet contrary views and understandings is one aspect of what I'm calling the *contrarium*. We can also think of it as a state or clearing in which contraries are held in suspension, a state of inbetweeness, an attentive unknowing in which polarities arise and are observed without comment or judgement. The *contrarium* can also be thought of as a bowl or vessel in which possibilities that may be diametrically opposed are held in a "coincidence of opposites", to use Nicholas of Cusa's term. (see McFarlane 2004)

One characteristic of the *contrarium*, as I envisage it, is that its dynamic polarities are never resolvable through the formulaic discourses of rationalism or dualism. In relation to the self as a manifestation of the *contrarium*, the polarities can only be handled by remaking the self as open work or work-in-progress. In this way the self can be considered as a dialectical process of construction, deconstruction and reconstruction – the self as an open-ended process rather than as a fixed unitary essence.

The *contrarium* is the space in which we pivot between the conflicting demands of opposing meanings, interpretations and ways of living, and negotiate the uncertain territory between self and other. And these divergencies or tensions have to be dealt with within a subjectivity that is experienced as having many currents or strands rather than as having a singular nucleus or centre. Indeed to seek for a fixed essence or purity is to misunderstand the way we, and all entities, are constituted. For reality is a confluence of identities and subjectivities, as impermanent and indeterminate as wind and cloud, and to be precise we are neither this nor that, neither one thing nor another – yet we are also this *and* that, self *and* other.

To develop these strands of thought, in this chapter I'm going to discuss ideas drawn from Roland Barthes, Theodor Adorno, Samuel Beckett, the Jain tradition of Indian philosophy, Leonardo da Vinci and G.K. Chesterton.

Observation XI – balancing in the park

I'm in a city park watching the world go by. A group of boys are kicking a ball about, as if they're not quite sure whether to play a game of football or to go on to something more exciting. Five girls sit and stand around a wooden bench, smoking and chatting very self-consciously about other girls who are absent from the group. As they talk and argue and laugh, they shoot glances at the boys and follow the movements of the ball, and the legs that kick it, with carefully disguised, yet intense, interest. At a line of swings two mothers push their toddlers in a gentle fashion as they talk about school and food and husbands. Under a shelter, painted with layered graffiti, a girl and a boy argue and shout and lose themselves in a tumult of accusation and pain. For them, this is a place and time of crisis, a showdown in which words are hurled like spears and no quarter seems to be given. From time to time everyone nearby turns to catch a glimpse of a relationship that's out of kilter, on the edge of distress and dissolution. It's an overcast gloomy day in early spring. A lone daffodil stands open-mouthed in the midst of a bed of wallflowers still grey and bedraggled from a season of frost and rain.

Right in front of me there's an ancient iron seesaw, painted pillar-box red, with a heavily greased axle at the centre of its bulky frame. A boy, who seems much too old to be doing what he's doing, stands with his legs apart balancing at the centre of the device. Although he's big and looks very strong, he's finding it difficult to keep from falling off. He maintains his position by constantly shifting his weight from one foot to the other, a series of delicate, hardly perceptible movements. He is intently focused on what he's doing, attending to every shift of weight and to every contraction and relaxation of muscle.

There is something of the ballet dancer about him, a gracefulness that belies his bulk. In the noise and fractiousness of this corner of the park he is a model of calm equanimity.

Barthes', *The Neutral*

If we turn to what was Roland Barthes' last book, *The Neutral*, (the first French edition was published posthumously in 2002) we find him pointing to or nudging us towards, an understanding of his term, the Neutral. In this collection of lecture notes and annotations Barthes draws on a diverse array of sources including: Daoism, John Cage, German mysticism, Pyrrhonist scepticism and Zen Buddhism. Although he doesn't outline in any detail a dialectical method, his approach to thinking and values involves both a critique of dualism and false dichotomies and the use of a sceptical dialectical process as an agency of critique. For instance, in discussing scepticism he writes: "Philosopher or not, man speaks by contradicting what others say and there is no way of deciding between them. Now, from the fact that the reasons are 'equivalent' [...] the sceptics (Timon) infer silence (*aphasia*)" – a silence he relates to "mystical silence". (Barthes 2005: 25) He also quotes Jean-Paul Dumont on *aphasia*:

> When a skeptic chooses to remain silent, he isn't searching for a comfortable refuge in the midst of doubt or for a means of avoiding error. To the contrary, he is only reflecting the state of balance of his soul when confronted with uncertain representations and submitted to equal contrary forces'. (ibid)

Towards the end of *The Neutral* (ibid: 211) he writes: "we have defined as pertaining to the Neutral every inflection that, dodging or baffling the paradigmatic, oppositional structure of meaning, aims at the suspension of the conflictual basis of discourse". This is reminiscent of the Madhyamika injunction to relinquish the habit of conceptualizing reality through discourse in dualistic terms.

Barthes (ibid: 27) argues in favour of Pyrrho's scepticism, which he describes as "pragmatic, antisystematic [...] a kind of signpost". For Barthes, it is equally "reasonable" to say either yes or no, or to keep silent, so long as we do not believe in, or attach ourselves, to either affirmation, negation or silence, or that we believe we are saying anything true or absolute or essential. That is, we shouldn't be systematic or emphatic in our statements, for, he points out, one should not "oppose dogmatic speech" with an "equally dogmatic silence". (ibid: 28) We need to be nimble-footed, non-attached, ambivalent, contrary, seeing the value, or lack of value, in all positions and to suspend judgment as far as possible. Barthes presents his positionless position – *the Neutral* – as an antidote to dogmatism, which he considers, like the sceptics before him, as the scourge of humanity, the source of much conflict and the antithesis of philosophical reason.

Adorno's negative dialectics

In his book *Negative Dialectics*, (1973) Theodor Adorno argues that one of the main purposes of his dialectical method is to strip away all sense of categorical identities, essential truths (however provisional) and theoretical definites. He considers indefiniteness, or what he calls "non-identity", and contradictoriness, to be integral qualities of reality. There are obvious echoes here of similar ideas in mystical writings and in the thinking of the Greek and later sceptics.

I'm going to focus on Adorno's introduction to *Negative Dialectics*, particularly those sections in which he first outlines his dialectical thinking. Though there are passing references to scepticism, implicitly critical, in a couple of footnotes, I don't know to what extent Adorno was familiar with the scepticism of classical Greece.

It seems to me that Adorno considers one of the main purposes of his dialectical method is to strip away all sense of categorical identities, essential truths (however provisional) and theoretical definites. He argues that while traditional western philosophy has used a variety of dialectical methods to identify or construct positive ideas, positions, theories or identities, "negative dialectics" has no such purpose. Indeed even negative dialectics itself is not to be considered as a theoretical standpoint, but rather as a method for establishing or realising the fluidity and indefiniteness of all standpoints or identities – a method for demonstrating that no concept or standpoint constitutes an essential truth or autonomous identity. Thus all truths, standpoints and theories imply or invite contradiction. By implication, indefiniteness, what

Adorno calls "non-identity", and contradictoriness are integral qualities of reality – whatever kind of cognitive field we take "reality" to
be. As he writes: "Contradiction is nonidentity under the rule of a law
that effects the nonidentical as well". (1973: 6)

One aspect of Adorno's critique of Hegel is that Hegel uses dialectics
to establish or construct "substantive or essential" knowledge, whereas for Adorno, if we are to practice philosophy (and to live) in the
light of the belief that there are no substantive essences, contents or
identities, then we have to give up "the illusion that [philosophy]
might confine the essence in its finite definitions". (ibid: 13) Adorno
urges us "not to play this game" of choosing between Yes and No,
True or False, as if these qualities or attributes are absolutes or fixed
essences. (ibid: 32) He also argues that:

> Dialectics is as strictly opposed to [relativism] as to absolutism; but it does not
> seek a middle ground between the two; it opposes them [both] through the ex-
> tremes themselves, convicts them of untruth by their own ideas. (ibid: 35)

This is very similar to the methodological claims of sceptics like Pyrrho and Sextus Empiricus.

Adorno recognises that, as he puts it, "A dialectics no longer 'glued'
to identity will provoke either the charge that it is bottomless […] or
the objection that it is dizzying". (ibid: 31) But Adorno seems to value
dizziness or vertigo as a positive quality: "In great modern poetry,
vertigo has been a central feeling since Baudelaire" (ibid) and this
vertigo is an "*index veri*" – an index of truth – which is often accompanied by "the shock of inconclusiveness". (ibid: 33) So the dizzying
feeling we get from engaging with the work of Baudelaire, Ezra
Pound, James Joyce or Anish Kapoor may be the result of the fact that
these makers realise in their work the flux of nonidentity, cutting the
threads that bind us to fixed or essential viewpoints and understandings. As Adorno writes, negative dialectics does "not come to rest in
itself" – that is, it is always at play, resisting at every turn, reification
and the craving for conclusions or answers which, in a sense, is the
antithesis of art. As we stand on the centre of the seesaw, keeping our
balance is a constant process of oscillating movements, our weight
moving this way and that.

Leonardo da Vinci's *sfumato*

At this point I'd like to draw attention to some of the implications of Leonardo da Vinci's term *sfumato*, (from the Italian, *fumo*, meaning smoke) particularly in relation to ideas about ambiguity, indeterminacy, boundlessness and process, all of which are central to Leonardo's interdisciplinary research.

In his copious writings about art Leonardo returns again and again to the theme of shadows and the countless ways in which forms are seen and can be depicted. In Precepts of the Painter, he writes: "The boundaries of bodies are the least of all things […] Therefore, O painter, do not surround your bodies with lines". (MacCurdy B 1956: 267) Elsewhere in his notes on philosophy (MacCurdy A 1956: 73-74) he ponders on the nature of the boundary between an entity and the *nothingness* which surrounds it, arguing that the boundary is common to both entity and space and is therefore not a boundary at all but a form of nothingness. This boundlessness is a characteristic of all existing entities. This belief manifests itself in the visual soft-edges and merging of forms in Leonardo's paintings and drawings, the use of smoky shadows making it difficult to discern where one form ends and another begins. It is also manifested in Leonardo's thinking which is open-ended, multi-facetted and inter-disciplinary, and more often than not about process, action and change rather than about static bodies and fixed truths. The much commented-upon unfinishedness of his work can also be seen as an inevitable manifestation of this strand of ideas and beliefs. (see also Kemp 2001: 97, 210-211)

In relation to Pyrrhonist scepticism, Madhyamika Buddhism, Adorno's "non-identity" and Barthes' "the *Neutral*" we have seen how distinctive dialectical methods are used to interrogate and destabilise essentialist dogmas. In this regard there are parallels with Leonardo's ideas about ambiguity and boundlessness – for underlying the concept of *sfumato* is a belief that there are no fixed or unitary essences to entities of any kind, including things or apparently solid objects. From Leonardo's point of view the world in which he found himself was a world of process, flux and evanescence – hence his preoccupation with the dynamics of water and wind, and his interest in machines which harness natural forces and movements to achieve particular goals.

Leonardo can be considered as an exemplary sceptical enquirer. The importance he attaches to the term *sfumato* arises from his belief in the absence of boundaries, the open-endedness of consciousness and cognition, and the flux of existence. He applies his understanding not only in his paintings, in which objects are depicted as having no perceptible edge or limit, but also in his open-minded thinking about the world – a world of process, change and inter-connectedness. These ideas and beliefs are also manifested in different ways in the works of many contemporary artists who make works that present us with a coincidence of opposites in which truth is always plural, bifurcated, multi-facetted and diamond-like. Examples include: Jannis Kounellis, Marina Abramovic, Martin Creed and John Cage – whose work is discussed in Part VI. One of the effects of these kinds of artworks is that they often bring us to a mental clearing – a lightening of mind and being, in which we realise that there are no fixed essences or essential truths but only a network of interdependent possibilities and meanings open to endless reformulation and change.

Observation XII – owl and stars

The way a misty evening shrouds us into night. Everywhere a quietness – except for dripping trees, a hooting owl and the dim stars muttering for a thousand light years.

Nothing is the way it is. Neither this nor that. Yes and no. It is, yet it is not

Samuel Beckett: "I take no sides"

It's interesting to note that Samuel Beckett repeatedly claimed that he tried to take no particular stance towards his characters and what they say or mean. In the early novel, *Watt*, he writes, "no symbols where none intended" and the director, Alan Schneider (1979: 173) reports Beckett as saying: "I take no sides. I am interested in the shape of ideas. There is a wonderful sentence in Augustine: 'Do not despair; one of the thieves was saved. Do not presume; one of the thieves was damned.' That sentence has a wonderful shape. It is the shape that matters". We could interpret this is as arguing for a kind of formalism, the sound and shape of the words and sentences as structurally meaningful, as formally autonomous. However that may be, at another level Beckett seems to be suggesting both a kind of symmetry in our relationships to things and a "suspension of judgement" (*epoche*) in relation to statements uttered: "I take no sides". About two of the main characters, Hamm and Clov, in *Endgame* he says: "Hamm as stated, and Clov as stated, together stated *nec tecum nec sine te* [neither with you nor without you], in such a place, and in such a world, that's all I can manage, more than I could". (in a 1957 letter to Schneider, quoted in Bair 1980: 39)

Terry Eagleton adds a coda to these thoughts about Beckett, suggesting that as truth is always indeterminate, language can only ever fail to convey the truth, but to borrow a Beckett phrase, "we have to keep trying to fail better". Eagleton goes on to mention that "Beckett once remarked that his favourite word was 'perhaps'". (Eagleton 2008: 9)

Observation XIII – magpies

A net has been hung, tightly-stretched, across and above a patch of waste ground. It is used by kids as a place in which to play badminton and hand-ball. A young magpie, raised earlier in the year in the ash tree nearby, lands on the top of the net. He clings to the wire as it lurches to and fro, using his long tail to keep balanced. Around him other magpies chatter and tussle, pecking at each other as they argue over a scrap of food on the ground. Every now-and-again a pair of crows joins in until, eventually, one of the burly crows flies away with the food. Yet still the magpies argue. Somehow the black and white bird trying to keep his balance on a quivering wire, reminds me of what we all might try to do – to keep our pied unsteady minds at a point of balance between competing points of view jostling to claim our allegiance.

Syadvada – the "maybe-so" doctrine

Within the many schools of Indian thought there lies another method of balancing the seesaw. Abraham Kaplan (1962: 230) mentions the term, *syadvada*, which is often used within the Jain tradition of Indian philosophy in relation to ideas of truth and philosophical arguments. *Syadvada*, is sometimes known as "the 'maybe-so' doctrine, or the doctrine of 'up to a point' or 'in a manner of speaking'". Kaplan suggests that according to this non-doctrinaire doctrine,

> No matter how carefully elaborated a philosophy may be, it remains, after all, only a human point of view. It is inseparable from a particular standpoint, and therefore inescapably expresses only a single perspective on a reality which transcends all perspectives. No proposition is wholly and completely true but only up to a point, in a manner of speaking. (ibid)

Kaplan argues that we shouldn't underestimate the implications of *syadvada*. It is not just that we can't decide as to what is true *or* false, or that all theories can offer only degrees of probability as to what is true or correct and, therefore, are never simply statements of fact. No, the more radical implication of *syadvada* is that we can only approach what we might call a true understanding of a particular state of affairs "not by choosing among alternative beliefs and philosophies, but by broadening our perspectives so as to find a place for the several alternatives". (ibid: 231) Taking account of different perspectives, however incompatible, is more likely to give us a more rounded, holistic, and probably more interesting and richer, understanding of a given phenomenon, than by selecting only one perspective and dogmatically asserting that this is "the truth".

The tendency of Indian religious practitioners and thinkers to consider all religions and philosophies as different *darśana*, or points of view, is a reflection of the desire to integrate, to synthesise and to find a position that encompasses competing, and possibly contradictory, alternatives. As Kaplan suggests, the truth "does not and cannot lie wholly on one side or the other, nor yet somewhere betwixt and between; what must be found is a larger perspective that incorporates both". (ibid: 232)

In the well-known Jain parable, the difficulty for the seven blind men who encounter an elephant for the first time is that none of them can stand back and gain a larger perspective that is inclusive of all their individual tactile experiences. That they can't also include a visual perspective only compounds the limitations in their knowledge. For one man, it is true that the leg of the elephant *is* like a tree. For another, the trunk *is* like a huge snake. And for another the tail is like a rope. But when they share their perspectives and attempt to describe or define what it is they have encountered, they can only guess on the basis of the evidence of their sense of touch, the spatial span of their arms (and, presumably the smell and sound of the animal). Whereas touching necessitates closeness, sight allows us to stand back, to walk around and to perceive at a distance. It is only when the blind men discuss their perspectives with each other and with others who have sight that both they and the sighted persons gain a more inclusive and deeper understanding of what that large, four-legged, snake-headed, thick-skinned, rope-tailed creature might be!

The theory of *Syadvada* is in many respects reminiscent of early Greek scepticism in its principles and in some of its dialectical methods. One similarity is in the way it analyses and evaluates any given proposition. According to the *Syadvada* system the truth value of any proposition can be considered from seven conditional perspectives:

1. *Syad-asti*—"in some ways it is"
2. *Syad-nasti*—"in some ways it is not"
3. *Syad-asti-nasti*—"in some ways it is and it is not"
4. *Syad-asti-avaktavyah*—"in some ways it is and it is indescribable"
5. *Syad-nasti-avaktavyah*—"in some ways it is not and it is indescribable"
6. *Syad-asti-nasti-avaktavyah*—"in some ways it is, it is not and it is indescribable"
7. *Syad-avaktavyah*—"in some ways it is indescribable"

Or, expressed in another way:

1. *Syad-asti*—Perhaps or maybe, it is
2. *Syat-nasti*—Perhaps or maybe, it is not
3. *Syad-asti nasti ca*—Perhaps or maybe, it is, it is not
4. *Syad-avaktavyah*—Perhaps or maybe, it is indeterminate or indescribable
5. *Syad-asti ca avaktavya sca*—Perhaps or maybe, it is and also indeterminate or indescribable
6. *Syat-nasti ca avaktavyasca*—Perhaps or maybe, it is not and also indeterminate or indescribable
7. *Syadasti nasti ca avaktav-yasca*—Perhaps or maybe, it is and it is not and also indeterminate or indescribable (Anon 2010a)

This evaluative process is called, *Saptabhangi*, "seven-fold predication" and is used to place any proposition in its conditional context and to avoid the fallacy of dogmatism – another similarity to scepticism. (ibid) For the Jain, there can be, and there are, many apparently competing, and possibly contradictory, truth values to any statement. There can be no absolute or essential truths, only conditional truth values within a relative scale.

The concepts of *Syadvada* and *Saptabhangi* relate to one of the basic principles of Jain philosophy, *Anekāntavāda*, which is closely connected to *Ahimsa* (non-violence). The term, *Anekāntavāda*, means "non-absolutism," and the recognition of this principle leads the Jain to accept and embrace relativism and pluralism – the belief that truth and reality are perceived differently from different points of view, and no single point of view is, or can be, the complete truth. Expressed in another way this means that all viewpoints are worthy of respect and need to be taken account of if we are to gain understanding. The belief that there is, or can be, one absolute or essential truth is dogmatism and is contrary to the Jain principle of *Ahimsa*, "avoidance of violence or injury". Thus for the Jain it is important to respect and to study other philosophies and belief systems, and not to do violence or injury, *himsa*, within the sphere of ideas. Intellectual *himsa*, so often leads to physical conflict, social disturbance or even war. The adversarial mode of argument, so typical of much contemporary debate (the "battle of ideas") is anathema to the Jain practice of *Ahimsa*. (ibid)

The Jain, alongside Buddhists, the early Greek sceptics, Michel de Montaigne and many mystics prefer not to attach themselves to one side or another in an argument, or to put it another way, try to understand *all* sides in a debate, in this way they exercise tolerance, generosity and respect for all beliefs – for all beliefs and assertions are interdependent and can only ever provide a small part of a larger picture.

Observation XIV – waves and ocean

Emerson's Hotel, Zanzibar, 1997. It is early morning. I look out through a fine wooden screen over a narrow balcony, across the multi-angled corrugated tin roofs, the green, yellow and re-painted spire of the Hindu temple, out over more tin roofs and the Christian church tower to the speckled waters of the bay where container ships, creaking old cargo vessels, dhows and ferries sit heavily in the brine. A choir of muezzins call from the many mosques, urging the faithful to rise for prayer. The Hindu temple bells are struck over and over again, rising in tempo and volume, until they suddenly stop. A pigeon flaps to the roof opposite, rests for a while and then flies away. Somewhere over the skeins of water lie Tanzania and the huge body of Africa. Down on the shore tiny waves nibble at coral rocks and a dark heron drags its tattered shadow over the dancing luminescence of the ocean.

G.K. Chesterton, paradox and surprise

Affinities with the Jain concept of *Syadvada* can be found in an unusual place – in the writings and dialectical methods of G.K. Chesterton – the half-forgotten eccentric metaphysician and author of the Father Brown stories. One word can simply characterise Chesterton's complex metaphysics: *paradox*. Chesterton, in his various guises as novelist, short-story writer, poet and Catholic apologist, explores the supreme paradox: that the Many is One; and, the One is Many. He is a masterful logician and sceptical believer who uses reason to undo reasonable assumptions.

As Hugh Kenner (1948: 65) notes: "If [Chesterton] saw two truths that seemed to contradict each other, he would take the two truths and the contradiction along with them". There would be no question of trying to reduce the complex paradoxes of existence to what he considered to be reasonable but illogical platitudes. A lamppost is both a hard metal object *and* a field of light, a fact *and* a fiction, a mundane thing *and* an inexplicable mystery. Kenner again: "the world is a baffling place, incapable of being enmeshed in a phrase or a formula". (ibid: 21) Chesterton accepts that there are no fixed identities, he anticipates, in many ways, Adorno's idea of "non-identity". He sums up his own position thus:

> All the straight roads of logic lead to some Bedlam, to Anarchism or to passive obedience, to treating the universe as a clockwork of matter or else as a delusion of the mind. It is only the Mystic, the man who accepts the contradictions, who can laugh and walk easily through the world. (in Kenner: 66)

Chesterton can be seen as using a dialectics of paradox to confront and explore the sheer fact of being, a fact which is unsettling and reassuring in equal measure. The creator of Father Brown is also an advocate and practitioner of a kind of mysticism of surprise – surprise that the world is as it is and that we should be here to experience it. He seems often to be simultaneously puzzled, full of wonder and amused by the sheer fact of existing. As Kenner writes, Chesterton considered "the world [to be] a baffling place, incapable of being enmeshed in a phrase or formula". (ibid: 21) He approaches things, even the things he has encountered many times before, as if for the first time. He sees with a critical and analytical eye, yet he is curiously innocent, without expectations or assumptions to cloud his vision. As he writes in an essay entitled, Heretics:

> All genuine appreciation rests on a certain mystery of humility and almost of darkness [...] The man who expects nothing sees redder roses than common men can see [...] Blessed is he that expecteth nothing, for he shall possess the cities and mountains. (ibid: 19)

Silhouette: John Bunyan

I lighted   I fell into a burning   I was a little overcome
I was walking into a wilderness   all words to dust did
chafe the air   miseries & wants were puddled into
a drought, as if my own light did drown them   a small
rain of joy did rise   I was dreamed into a stone & into
a melting & lost all skinfolded form into this shimmering
these rags of words are not enough   how would it be
to touch you into what it is   how to put fingers to eternity
or to swim with the void   neither here nor there nor doubting
nor any certainty nor any ashes of this quick fire   it is
& I am shadowed by its light

[Composed from fragments of John Bunyan's, *To Be a Pilgrim*]

the art
of not
knowing

and so it is
this writing
a ghostly making

Part VI

Living with uncertainty: art and its making

> "All I know is that I know nothing".
> Socrates.
> (in Bakewell 2010: 124)

> "My footing is so unsteady and so insecure".
> Michel de Montaigne.
> (ibid)

Introduction

In this chapter I present some ideas about uncertainty and contingency in relation to daily living and to the making of art. Although I have discussed and made reference to various artists and poets elsewhere in these notes, at this point I am going to focus in more detail, though still in brief, on particular artists and poets, and a few examples of their work – tracing some ideas about art as a mode of action and process, a way of doing, knowing and being.

Living with uncertainty

Few things are more certain than that uncertainty is integral to our lives. We engage with unavoidable uncertainties from the moment we are born to the uncertain moment that we die. We don't know whether or when we will become ill; whether and when we will get well; what results we will get in our exams or how successful we will be in our careers; how much money we will make or how much we will lose; whether or not we will meet the love of our life; what the weather will be like in four weeks time; whether the dice we have thrown will yield a six; or if tomorrow will bring good news or bad. These are imponderables that we have to live with. Uncertainty is an inevitable consequence of living in a relational universe that is constantly changing in an indeterminate way.

However, we are often not very adept at dealing with uncertainty – indeed we seem to spend much of our lives trying to avoid or deny it, or to replace it with beliefs and speculations to which we cling with great tenacity. We construct elaborate narratives that purport to describe and explain how the world is, in such a way that we can feel secure in our knowledge and be certain in our relationships with the world. We attempt to defuse the problematic paradoxes and imponderables of our existence, which lie like landmines across our path. We do this either by pretending they are not there (not always a healthy strategy) or by finding ingenious ways of mine-sweeping that seem to offer us a zigzagging course of apparent safety. Put in very simple terms we seem to have two possible ways of dealing with the uncertainty we feel in relation to a reality that is in constant and unpredictable motion: we can either try to cling to something that gives us at least a temporary (if false) sense of security; or, we can let go and move with the fluid medium of existence – waking up to the way things are *in process*, subject to constant change.

In his recent writings about Buddhism, Stephen Batchelor (2010: 128-135) emphasises contingency as a condition of existence. The term, *contingency*, in a philosophical sense is useful in that it brings together three strands of meaning: one, "the condition of being free from necessity with regard to existence"; two, "openness to the effect of chance or free will"; and three, "uncertainty of occurrence". (see Anon 2002a: 501) While we can never know what will happen next on the road of life, we are in many ways free to believe, value and respond as we think fit with regard to what arises from moment-to-moment. Of course, what we believe and value is dependent upon how and what we learn, and how and what we are taught. Beliefs and values are formulated within particular historical, social and cultural contexts. We are all *free* only insofar as circumstances, and the opportunities open to us, allow.

The dialectical and contemplative methods of many sceptics and mystics, and the modes of enquiry of many artists and poets, can be considered as ways of becoming more fully aware of the contexts within which all of us live, and through critical awareness and interrogation they can open up the possibility of transforming who and how we are in the world. Hence the belief amongst many sceptics, mystics, artists and poets that the practice of a particular vocation can help the practitioner to become freer and more open – better able to perceive the way things are in the world and better able to determine how they respond to, and navigate through, life's uncharted waters. By attending to and working with the unavoidable contingency of existence, rather than trying to deny or avoid it, we may be able to deal more effectively with the surprises, snags, pleasures and pains that lie just around the next corner. Or, more importantly we may come to realise that whatever lies around the next corner we first have to deal with what lies *before* the next corner, that is what is here and now. In attempting to attend to what is *here* in all its relational and contingent glory, mystics and sceptics contribute something very distinctive and important to our understanding of how we can all live richer and less troubled lives.

Artists and poets as agents of uncertainty

In this section I will suggest some parallels and connections between the ideas and actions of mystics and sceptics and the work of a number artists and poets who can also be considered as agents of uncertainty.

The sceptics whose ideas I have discussed in these pages use all kinds of methods, especially a remorseless kind of dialectical analysis, to expose the contradictions, paradoxes and nonsense inherent in taking any particular side in an argument or in making any kind of dogmatic assertion that poses as a truth or fixed statement about the essence of things. Sceptical enquiry is always in motion, open to revision, reformulation and new possibilities.

Likewise the work, and works, of many artists and poets can be considered as manifesting similar qualities of openness of enquiry and a kind of ungraspability as to meaning and status. Artworks tend to resist definition (as does art itself) and tend to be quite amenable to competing, conflicting and contradictory opinions. In experiencing and engaging with works of art we are liberated from the dictatorship of unitary meanings or single truths. To get the most out of artworks (and maybe out of life) we have to try to be nimble-footed, non-

attached to fixed positions, agile of mind, sensuously receptive, ambivalent and contrary. We have to find ways in which to embrace uncertainty and complexity, and to be able to play with many meanings
and multiple interpretations. This playfulness involves both *epoché*,
"suspension of judgement" and *aphasia*, "freedom from linguistic
categories", and it is this liberating, challenging, and at times deeply
disturbing, playing with ideas, values, beliefs, imaginings and doings,
that contributes to the power and significance of art.

This position-less position should not be mistaken as "sitting on the
fence". It is rather that there are no fences upon which to sit (because
there are no essential boundaries or definitions as the sceptics might
say). The important strategy is to be open to all possibilities and to
maximise opportunities for possibilities to be open to others.

It could be argued that the sceptic and artist (and I would suggest
many mystics) are involved in what Umberto Eco calls, *open work* – a
working with, and gathering together of, particular materials, ideas,
narratives and images that have no fixed meanings or interpretations.
(see Eco 1989) In this kind of open work we are at play – in the sense
that we have no predetermined goal. Playing with ideas, images and
materials, we may suspend critical, analytical and rationalistic processes in order to see what happens, to let things develop in ways
which accommodate chance, randomness and intuition. As an artist I
know that periods of working *in the dark*, or when *not sure of what is
happening*, can be as exciting and productive as periods of lucid control. In any creative process unlearning and stepping outside the formulaic constraints of acquired skills can release new ways of thinking
and making. These situations are highly complex and unstable, requir-
ing flexible thinking and responsive handling of material processes.
Meaning and making are in a state of flux, with countless possibilities
rapidly presenting themselves. Developing the ability to improvise
(with ideas as well as materials), and to generate and make use of
situations in which indeterminacy and contingency prevails, are key
aspects of enquiry within art.

This way of thinking about art as an open work leads to a revision in
the way we think about artist, artwork and audience. The audience is
no longer to be considered as a relatively passive receiver or observer

of the work but rather as an active participant in the realisation of the work's unfolding in the world. The art*work*, or the *work* of art, involves an activity, a doing, a working with *something* – a weaving of strands of meaning out of an engagement with a substance in a space – this is as true of the audience as of the artist. This interpretative activity complements the work of the artist, who acts as both an agent of uncertainty and as an agent of meaning-making. The making of the artwork is *always* a collaborative participatory process – something creative happening *between* artist, material and anyone who engages with, or in, the work. And this being *in* the work, or being *at* work, is exciting and enriching. We find ourselves playing with meanings, happy to hold in mind contradictory interpretations and to enjoy suspending judgements about which is the right view. We accept, for a time, both this *and* that, as being equally valid – a *contrarium* or "coincidence of opposites" as Nicholas of Cusa might describe it.

We can think of the sites of art, as sites of learning and enquiry, as overlapping hermeneutical fields – spaces or arenas in which multiple interpretations arise, jostling against each other. Sometimes there may be a fusion of interpretations, a provisional convergence of understandings or analyses, but just as often there may be a dynamic divergence between interpretations that are incommensurable or contradictory – we cannot determine what is right or wrong, true or false, because each interpretation is as valuable, useful or enjoyable as another. And this polysemic and non-hierarchical state can be productive, stimulating and highly creative – a state of open-ended learning. It is a condition to be valued and sustained for as long as possible – a non-dogmatic holding in mind of many possibilities. But once we focus on one or other of the multiple possibilities we leave the "coincidence of opposites" for a more dogmatic state of knowing and being.

In our engagements with artworks we are often confronted with the presence or *beingness* of objects or materials – a state of actuality that is neither this nor that, *neti neti*, yet also this *and* that, a *contrarium* in which truth is always plural, bifurcated, multi-facetted and diamond-like. Artworks are very beneficial partly because they often bring us to a mental clearing – a lightening of mind and being, in which we realise that there are no fixed essences or essential truths but only a network of interdependent possibilities and potentialities open to endless reformulation and change. We find art exciting and revitalising in so far as we become open to many equal and contradictory meanings – all *and* none of which are true. In being open to many truths we are liberated from the dictatorship of one truth, and are thus empowered. It is to be regretted that we tend not to carry these ways of thinking and being out of the art gallery or concert hall and use them to live with the conflicts and uncertainties that confront us in the complex uncertain world outside.

It seems to me that art is a mode of philosophical enquiry. The arts can be seen as presenting us with a long history of metaphysical investigation and celebration through symbolic encoding, experiential analysis and cultural experiment. Countless artists have, and do, conduct ontological enquiries through material presence and symbolic notation. They question, analyse and celebrate what it is to be. What it is to exist in a continuum of being and becoming that stretches from the rudimentary light processing of microscopic algae and amoeba, to the cultural processing of more complex organisms including plants, animals and humans, to the information processing of digital technologies and other extensions of human consciousness.

When the philosopher, Thomas Nagel, poses the question, "what is it like" to be this or that? (see Nagel 1979) he is also indirectly affirming the importance of the arts to philosophical enquiry – in that the arts endlessly pose this kind of question and provide us with countless equally valid and varied responses or realisations to such questions. Artists present us with complex material and symbolic enactments of what it is to inhabit this particular space, to be embodied minds interacting with other embodied minds (beings, artefacts, buildings, habitats, histories, cultures), what it is to be both flesh and bone, and light and energy-processing consciousness.

The arts are remarkably effective at forming and exploring these ideas and questions in ways that are non-totalising, reflexively critical, non-dogmatic, multi-valent and non-reductive. It could be argued that one important function of the arts is the realisation of thought, feeling and experience in open artworks that are both materially specific and infinitely interpretable or indeterminate. In this sense artworks manifest qualities that are reassuring and concrete as objects and processes, while at the same time being subversive and uncertain as to value and meaning. Without being didactic in any overt or formulaic way, artworks can be seen as sites of open-ended learning and analytical enquiry – modes of interrogation as well as modes of celebration – *showing* us something of the changeful, contradictory, relational nature of reality.

Showing rather than telling

Dogen's use of the term *dōtoku* [see p. 126 above] to refer to both expression and the immanence of expression within all actions and situations, brings to mind an interesting aspect of the relationship between philosophical ideas and art. In Dogen's pedagogic methods and in the activities of other Buddhist teachers we come across many examples of how showing can be just as effective as telling in bringing a student to a realisation of some facet or other of Buddhist ideas and practice. In the Zen tradition the importance of doing, showing and demonstrating insight can be traced back to the well-known story of the Buddha showing a gathering of students a lotus flower. As he holds it in silence before his audience, one of his followers, Mahākāśyapa, smiles gently. Buddha interprets the single fleeting smile as a manifestation of Mahākāśyapa's intuitive realisation of the Buddha's teachings. Buddha is then supposed to have addressed his students by reminding them that his teachings are not dependent on words or letters – he is not teaching an academic discipline or a theory, instead he is showing them how to cope with the trials and tribulations of everyday life. Buddhism, the middle way, is a special transmission outside of the scriptures. As a way of being, knowing and doing, it has to be passed from person to person, using whatever methods come to hand. Transmission by words is only one of these methods or *dōtoku*. Actions, expressions, gestures, including silence and holding up a flower, are others. Needless to say Buddha entrusts to Mahākāśyapa the task of transmitting his teachings to others.

In the literature of Zen there are many examples of teachers demonstrating their teachings in non-verbal gestures and bringing students to realisation through actions. These range from the bizarre: Bodhidharma, who is credited with bringing Chan (Zen) Buddhism from India to China, tearing off his eyelids after falling asleep in his seventh year of meditating facing a wall in a cave; or, Bodhidharma's disciple, Huike, cutting off his own left arm to prove to Bodhidharma how committed he was to his studies – to the more prosaic: Hakuju, a nineteenth century Japanese Zen teacher, noticing on a hot day that his students were beginning to fall asleep during one of his lecture, puts down his lecture notes, settles himself comfortably in his chair and falls deeply asleep himself; or, the Chinese aristocrat, Yasuoki, as a young man, meeting Bankei, the famous Zen master, deciding to catch him off-guard by flourishing his spear as if to run Bankei through, only to find that Bankei flicks aside the spear with his rosary, saying that Yasuoki is too worked up to handle his spear correctly. In later life, Yasuoki, by then a great spears-man, referred to Bankei as the one who had taught him most about his art. (see Stryk and Takashi 1965 for more anecdotes)

A connection can be traced between these examples of bringing someone to a realisation through action, or by using gesture and non-verbal means to disturb habits of thought and behaviour, and a strand of actions undertaken by contemporary artists. I'd like to discuss, very briefly, the work of a number of artists who seem to epitomise this mode of practice.

Marina Abramovic

Marina Abramovic was born in Yugoslavia ("a country that no longer exists", as she once said) in 1946. She has been making performance works since the late 1960s. Abramovic has been involved with Tibetan Buddhist communities in India since 1979, often working with them to choreograph the dancing and chanting of monks or to develop her own work in new ways. (Baas & Jacob 2004: 188) In *Nightsea Crossing – Conjunction*, 1983, she invited a Tibetan Buddhist monk and an aborigine medicine man from Central Australia to join Abramovic herself and her artist-collaborator, Ulay, to sit in silence on opposite sides of a table for four days in four-hour sessions. According to Abramovic this was the first contact between Aboriginal and Tibetan cultures. The gallery visitors see the four motionless figures – they can sense the flow of energy within and between them but cannot know what they are experiencing. It is very unsettling to closely observe four human beings manifesting such stillness, concentration and discipline without being given an explanation or reason for their behaviour.

In another well-known work from 1980, titled *Rest Energy*, Abramovic and Ulay stand opposite each other. Ulay holds an arrow notched on to the taut string of a powerful bow held with one hand by Abramovic. They both lean outwards, their weight adding tension to the primed bow. The tip of the arrow points at Abramovic's chest only a few inches away. Both artists sway in unison, the sound of their breathing as they hold position and keep the tension steady can be clearly heard in a video clip of the action. (see Abramovic 1980) They maintain their stance for as long as they are able – pushing themselves to the limit. In this work there is undoubted danger – one brief lapse of attention and the string could slip out of Ulay's fingers, releasing the arrow with potentially severe consequences. As we watch we can sense the danger, feel the heightened awareness of the two artists and wonder at what possesses them to do something so extreme – let alone to do it in the name of art in a gallery setting.

While Abramovic talks about the intense shifting states of consciousness that she experienced in these pieces – similar to experiences she has had while in meditation – we, as an audience, can only guess at what is going on. We wonder at the stamina of the participants, the fact that they can sit or stand for so long in the face of such public scrutiny and yet retain their composure. We may feel a kind of admiration combined with curiosity and uncertainty as to how to make sense of what is happening in front of us. Yet, although there is no obvious closure to the questions unfolding in our minds, no answers or solutions, we go away intrigued, oddly excited by the feeling of *not knowing* what is going on.

Jannis Kounellis

I'm sitting in my studio wondering where to go next with a drawing that never seems to be quite right. As so often happens I take down a book from the shelves behind me and flick through the pages until I find something that is both enticing and perplexing: a photograph of horses stabled in an art gallery. It is Rome, 1969. Jannis Kounellis, a Greek artist who has been based in Italy for much of his working life, is exhibiting the horses as art or as a question mark in the face of art. The work is untitled. The horses no doubt move, make horse noises and fill the air with horse smells. Buckets and a broom stand in the corner. Despite their residence in a gallery the horses resist categorisation as art. They pull at the ropes tethering them to the wall. The glare of gallery lights exposes every vein and mark on their skin.

We seek some resolution of our uncertainty. Questions keep coming to mind: why are they here? how are we expected to view them? what idea is the artist enacting? what does this spectacle mean? But there is nothing to help us. No explanation, title or commentary. All we have are 11 horses – being horses – tethered in a large, brightly lit, space. This unsettling conundrum is typical of Kounellis's work. There is something deeply intriguing about the objects and materials that he brings together in a space. We gaze at them, wander around them (if we're lucky enough to see an actual installation) and ponder on the significance of what we encounter. Although, as with all puzzles, we grapple with potential resolutions to our questions, unlike other kinds of finite puzzles we tend not to mind that we don't find "an answer", for there can be no answer. We walk away from the work somehow enlightened – in the sense that we aren't burdened with any particular meaning or answer, indeed we seem to have let go of our desire for certainty and singularity of interpretation. Instead we have enjoyed, and continue to enjoy, the uncertainty that the enigmatic work generates in us.

John Cage – waking-up:
self-construction rather than self-expression

The American composer, artist and writer, John Cage (1912-1992), in an interview with Daniel Charles, speaks of the relationship between art and the world-as-process:

> The world, the real is not an object. It is a process [...] The function of art at the present time is to preserve us from all logical minimizations that we are at each instant tempted to apply to the flux of events. To draw us nearer to the process which is the world we live in. (in Perloff 1996: 196-197)

This aspiration of Cage's, to draw near "to the process which is the world we live in", is stated in a slightly different way when he quotes Coomaraswamy's injunction that art should "imitate nature in her manner of operation" – a phrase Cage comes back to many times in his writings and conversations. (see Cage 1966: 194) The artist's job is not to express his- or her-self, but to generate structures that approximate to the processes that operate in nature. These structures are complex, usually made up of many linear determinate strands, interwoven and layered in such a way that the unfolding totality is an indeterminate, highly complex, conglomeration of forces and constituent parts. As Perloff (1996: 202) puts it, Cage sees "'self-discipline' as a way of displacing 'self-expression' from the romantic tradition of the artist as self-centred seer". Discipline is needed to fulfil Cage's "repeated insistence that 'art is not an attempt to bring order out of chaos [...] but simply a way of waking up to the very life we're living,

which is so excellent once one gets one's mind and one's desire out of
its way and lets it act of its own accord'".

Cage works to make the ego more porous and transparent, to let the
light pass through a skin that is a mediating membrane rather than an
inviolable barrier. The distinction between "inside" and "outside", self
and world, is blurred and reduced, such that in Cage's music, writing
and performance, the individual is considered and treated as a participant in the world (and in the work), not as an entity separate from the
world. As participants *in* the world, in the music, writing and performance, we have to be awake to what is happening all around us, we
have to be responsive, critical and questioning, alive to whatever arises in consciousness. Cage (1981: 239) likens this aliveness and atten-
tiveness to a kind of liberation: "Among these wanderings – and *in the
middle of them* – here, all of a sudden, is a release. Or an opening".
The language used here is reminiscent of Eckhart and Heidegger –
Gelassenheit, a release or "letting-be"; *Dasein*, the openness of "being-here". [see p.27 above]

Bill Viola

The American artist, Bill Viola, is renowned for his video works,
which are crafted with the care and technical resources more usually
associated with feature films. Viola has had a long-standing interest in
Buddhist ideas and practices and his work can be seen as being informed by these interests. Viola is very articulate in describing the
emergence of his ideas and about the ways in which ideas are realised
in audio-visual form. Here is an example of Viola describing an inci-
dent that had a considerable impact on him; it presents some similarities to the accounts provided by Thomas Merton and other writers of
"mystical" experiences which were turning points in their lives. [eg.
Brother Lawrence, see p. 45 above] Often grounded in the humdrum
routines of everyday life, these accounts combine an almost breathless
intensity with great precision and clarity.

> I was walking home one rainy evening in New York City and I had to stop briefly
> to wipe the raindrops off my eyeglasses. As I held my glasses up to clean them, a
> car drove by and I instantly noticed the image of its headlights passing through all
> the tiny raindrops clinging to the surface of my lenses. I looked closer. Another

car went by. I could clearly see within each droplet a perfect little image of the street [.....] I looked around and saw that the water drops on the hood of a parked car were also imaging the street scene. I realised, in fact, that every drop of water, even the falling rain, was doing the same [.....] these images were not reflections, but were optical images. Each waterdrop was functioning as a tiny wide-angle lens to image the world around [.....] I raced back to my studio, got out my video camera and began to experiment with magnifying the image in the waterdrop. (Viola 1995: 41)

Viola goes on to relate how out of this experience he developed one of his best known early works, Migration, made in 1976, which includes images of a room seen through the fish-eye lens of a drop of water. Viola is alive to what is going on in his field of perception. He becomes aware of something that he hadn't noticed before. He observes this phenomenon closely, takes note of its qualities and explores the implications of what he has seen with the technology he has to hand (a video camera). On another occasion he describes the particular mode of awareness out of which his ideas often emerge:

[.....] field perception is the awareness or sensing of an entire space at once. It is based on a passive, receptive position, as in the way we perceive sound, rather than an aggressive, fragmented one, as in the way our eye works through the narrowing function of focused attention. (ibid: 151-152)

What Viola is describing here seems very similar to the state of attention we have noted in relation to *zazen* and mindfulness, attending to the whole relational field of awareness – trying to observe without judgement or commentary. While Viola takes this state of awareness as both a starting point and as a model for how his completed works function in relation to his audience, other artists can be considered as employing this state of awareness as an integral part of their working method.

Antonio López Garcia

One example of this method can be seen in the work of the Spanish painter, Antonio López Garcia, who was born in 1937. His paintings, drawings and sculptures are all produced as a consequence of a very slow exacting process of observation and representation. López Garcia nearly always works directly from the subject, which may be a person he knows, the panorama of Madrid seen from a nearby hill or the left-overs of a family meal. Whatever his subject López Garcia is concerned with visual interrogation, examining in a dispassionate and accurate way what arises in the whole visual field. His work involves two main strands of enquiry: the activities of perceiving and of representing what is perceived.

I sit now with a photograph of a López Garcia drawing on the desk in front of me. The drawing is entitled, Remains of a Meal, and was made in 1971. (see Brutvan 2008:115) It represents part of a table-top as it appears after a meal has been eaten – or rather it represents the *sustained observation* of a bowl and a plate and their contents, a glass of water, a crumpled napkin, and other objects lying on a creased and stained white table-cloth. The drawing is made with a fairly hard graphite pencil, giving the whole image a silvery grey tonality with just a few dark areas. In the foreground subtle gradations of grey delineate the features of a bowl with various small bones, perhaps from a rabbit, opened sea-shells and a glistening spoon propped on the wide edge of the bowl. The whole image is quite modest in size (42 x 54 cms) and yet it is compositionally grand in scale – the pale areas of table-cloth giving a sense of space and light to the picture.

The orchestration of tones and forms suggests, paradoxically, both informality of subject-matter and formality of execution. This is an everyday, humdrum scene, observed with great care, even reverence. Some parts of the image hover on the edge of recognisability. The graphite is used to evoke edges and surfaces rather than to define them or pin them down. The water in the glass is in places indistinguishable from the space around it, the napkin may not be a napkin – its identity is uncertain, as if López Garcia was drawing something he'd never seen before. In the far top right-hand corner of the picture a group of forms blur into an indefinite jumble. Here and there erratic puddles of shadow suggest small chunks of bread and crumbs. The artist conveys sensory information without imposing a definitive reading.

Our perception of the drawing echoes the artist's perception of the subject. We are lead to scan the pictorial field in much the same way that López Garcia scans the remains of the meal, and the act of observing, without commentary and without interposing hierarchies of narrative order or symbolic value, is surprisingly similar to the practices of contemplative prayer or *zazen*. López García can be seen as continuing a long tradition of observational realism in Spanish art. With its roots in religious iconography, the depiction of saints and biblical scenes, the tradition gradually turned its attention to the objects and materials that were formerly part of the backdrop to a Christian story, bestowing upon the everyday world the same degree of contemplative scrutiny and reverence that had once been reserved only for the great characters and deeds of the church. López García brings us up close to the shifting uncertainties of perception and representation, reminding us that the most insignificant of things and events, is worthy of observance and quiet contemplation.

Ad Reinhardt

I'd now like to turn to a very different artist, who can be considered as exploring a very different aspect of contemplation and consciousness. The American painter, Ad Reinhardt (1913-1967), became famous, or perhaps notorious, for a number of series of so-called monochromatic and black paintings produced between the very late 1950s and his death in 1967. In many of these paintings Reinhardt deploys a range of black pigments, for black comes in as many subtle hues and tones as white or any colour in the spectrum. Just as López García, in his drawings, orchestrates a very limited palette of silver grey tones from light to dark, Reinhardt uses a restricted palette of blacks, subtly different in colour, tone and material quality (from shiny to matt). These variations in blackness, a relative absence of coloured light reflected from the surface of the painted canvas, are composed into very simple forms – for instance, a cross, or vertical or horizontal bands. As the viewer encounters a particular painting – moving nearer, stepping from side to side, scanning the pictorial field – he or she notices the subtle differences in tone, hue and surface, gradually coming to see what was at first hidden or unrecognised. In this brief encounter with the painting the viewer's sensibility is enhanced, their powers of observation and visual sensitivity are stretched and developed.

Reinhardt was almost as well-known for his writings about art as he was for his paintings. He was fond of making rather dogmatic assertions about the purposes of art and about the importance of art for the wider culture and society. He tended to place importance on the value of art as a counter to what he saw as the utilitarian, materialistic and acquisitive nature of American society. Reinhardt harangues the readers of art magazines with barbed criticisms of the follies of a life-style centred on the pursuit of wealth, fame and more of everything. Instead he argues for an art of absence and apparent emptiness – an art of less rather than more. In 1962 he writes: "The one thing to say about art is its breathlessness, lifelessness, deathlessness, contentlessness, formlessness, spacelessness, and timelessness. This is always the end of art". (Baas 2005: 125) On another occasion he urges his readers to look outside the western traditions of art for ways out of the cultural and social cul-de-sac into which he believes his contemporaries have driven: "The intensity, consciousness and perfection of Asiatic art comes from repetitiousness and sameness". (ibid. 126) He argued that only "complete awareness, disinterestedness" constituted the right state of mind in which to make and engage with art. We can relate this state of acute yet non-discriminatory awareness to the ideas of aesthetic disinterestedness advocated by the radical modernist artist, Marcel Duchamp, to the suspension of judgement practiced by Pyrrhonist sceptics and to the benign non-discriminatory observance of consciousness practiced by the Zen student who sits just to sit.

Reinhardt's black and seemingly monochromatic paintings are challenging in many ways, including the way in which we are confronted with our habitual need to look *for* something. The dense yet subtly reflective surfaces of his paintings resist our attempts to find a spatial bearing or an identifiable image within the pictorial field or a meaning within the semantic field. Reinhardt's quiet yet insistent works tend to draw us, often against our will, to a position in which all we can do is perceive what is before us, experiencing disorientation and uncertainty, and letting go for a while of our need to impose definitive structures and meanings. Just as our attempts to *solve* a *koan* by rationalisation and intellectual means are doomed to failure, so we only come to terms with Reinhardt's paintings by giving up our preconceptions and experiencing instead *what is here*. Reinhardt makes an art of the manifesto or polemical list, and usually his lists and rules for making art, are lists of what *not* to do. He advocates a strategy of elimination and erasure, in the spirit of the Christian, Jewish and Islamic mystics who thought that only by naming everything in the universe would you be left with what was unnameable: that is, Yahweh or God. In one of his last lists, Twelve Rules for a New Academy, 1957, he writes at the end: "The fine artist should have a fine mind, free of all passion, ill-will and delusion". (ibid. 131) It could have been written by a Buddhist teacher or an early Greek sceptic.

Martin Creed

Martin Creed is another artist who takes a less-is-more attitude, but he makes work that is radically different to the sombre paintings of Ad Reinhardt. Creed won the Turner Prize in 2001 and caused a great deal of controversy at the prize-winners exhibition that year. Since about 1987 Creed has numbered his works, often adding a title that refers to the material out of which the work is made, or to an obvious characteristic of the work. The piece he exhibited in 2001 is entitled, *Work No. 227, the lights going on and off*, and as the title indicates in an accurate deadpan way, the work consists of the lights going on and off in a timed sequence in one of the gallery spaces. Creed (2010) describes his works as pieces of theatre and the gallery space as a theatrical space – a place in which the artist can draw our attention to objects and occurrences that may be happening around us at any time but to which we pay little attention – a theatre of the everyday.

Creed (ibid) also likens his own work to music and many of the works can be activated or re-enacted by anyone using the title or an initial encounter with the work as a template for their own enactment of the piece – just as a musician might perform from a notational score. In relation to *Work No 227*, the experience of being in a room as the lights go on and off is not an unusual experience, it is a humdrum event, usually of no more significance than that we are entering or leaving a room. Creed takes this simple situation but gives it a theatrical twist which leaves us in a state of uncertainty or ambivalence about what is going on. Why is the light going on and off? Is there a regular or irregular pattern to the sequence? Is this the start of something, or its end? What is happening to our field of vision when we see a brief after-image as the light goes off? And what is happening as our eyes adjust first to the relative darkness of the space and then to its brightness? The work, with the simplest and least of means, draws our attention to a kind of in-between state, a state of indecision or uncertainty as to what to do and how to interpret or respond to what is happening. In some ways, we could see this work of Creed's as an exemplification of the idea of the *contrarium*. [see p. 151]

The artist himself, in a commentary on a video-clip of the work on his website (ibid), makes a link between the light going on and off and one of his songs, *I don't know what I want*. He suggests that the simple decision as to whether to have the lights on or off in the gallery space, presented him with a conundrum because he didn't know what he wanted. *Work No. 227*, like the song, takes the conundrum as its *raison d'être*, giving the indecision a tangible (and decisive) form. *Not knowing* what he wants can be seen as a positive state, a state of being open to possibilities, embracing uncertainty and attending to the present. Elsewhere Creed elaborates on this theme of not knowing, using a spare and enigmatic language that is reminiscent of Meister Eckhart, Jacob Boehme or Samuel Beckett.

> I don't know what I want to say, but, to try to say something, I think I want to try to think. I want to try to see what I think. I think trying is a big part of it, I think thinking is a big part of it, and I think wanting is a big part of it, but saying it is difficult, and I find saying trying and nearly always wanting. I want what I want to say to go without saying. (Creed 2001)

Creed's work can be seen as a development of the ideas and practices of John Cage, drawing our attention to everyday experiences and to the delights of being-in-the-world. It can also be considered as a way of posing unanswerable questions or moments of uncertainty – a questioning of habitual responses and formulaic behaviours. As such the artist can be viewed as both an agent of uncertainty and as a maker of works that heighten our awareness of the mysterious and contingent nature of ordinary events and situations.

Charles Wright

The American poet, Charles Wright, was born in Tennessee in 1935. During a long writing career he has returned again and again to the mysteries and delights of being alive and to what Willard Spiegelman

(2005: 82) refers to as, "the metaphysics of the quotidian". Wright, like many of the mystical writers I have been discussing, finds unfathomable paradoxes at the heart of existence: "Such emptiness at the heart, / such emptiness at the heart of being, / Fills us in ways we can't lay claim to, / Ways immense and without names". (Wright 2001: 14-15) This extract is from the poem, Cicada, in which Wright describes a morning of domestic restlessness, "opening books and closing books, / Sitting in this chair and that chair". This restlessness, apparently homely and inconsequential, underlies much of Wright's writing. His precise diction combines everyday language with occasional surprises – references to St. Augustine, Pascal, Chinese poets, Simone Weil and rather obscure terms such as "*apokatastatic*" (the Greek for renovation or restoration) – and often suggests a struggle to engage with states of mind and awareness that lie at the margins of what is nameable or expressible in language – "ways immense and without names". There are echoes here of Lao Tzu and Zen – both suggesting that showing can be more effective than telling, pointing and demonstrating can be more likely to lead to realisation than definition or description.

For Wright, actuality, the state of being here, is always beyond the grasping vocabulary of verbal language. He quotes Thomas Aquinas: "All I have written seems like straw / Compared to what I have seen and what has been revealed to me". (ibid: 157) This sense of always being one-step-behind his own awareness of life gives his writing an air of poignancy, an underlying regretful acceptance that writing, poetry, art will always be not quite up to the job of transcribing experience. His poetry seems always tinged with awareness of its own limits and unrealisable aspirations. Just as his "life keeps sliding out from under me, intact but / Diminishing", (ibid: 103) so his attempts at evoking that life in poetry leave him with a sense of dissatisfaction: "Everything that the pencil says is erasable". (ibid) In the same poem, Lives of the Saints, he refers to the Zen life as "contemplative, cloistered, tongue-tied", (ibid) and there is something of these qualities in Wright's persona as encountered in his poetry.

In the wrily titled, Poem Almost Wholly in my own Manner, Wright provides us with a glimpse of his own poetics: "Poetry's what's left between the lines – / a strange speech and a hard language, / It's all in the unwritten, it's all in the unsaid...". (ibid: 94) This is reminiscent of the *apophatic* tradition in mystical literature – the use of negation and an emphasis on what can't be said. Wright often appears to be ambivalent about the value of poetry as a way of distilling in words the experience of being alive. For Wright, poetry renders "strange" even everyday language, and we can interpret him as suggesting that poetic language, in his work, is difficult ("hard") and hewn in as concrete ("hard") a form as possible. While poetic language seems only able to wash against the shore of quotidian reality, Wright seems to feel his linguistic grappling with the ineffability of existence is nevertheless worthwhile: "that's a comfort, I think, / for our lack and inarticulation". (ibid)

In Wright's work we find a weaving together of an acute observing of what arises in the field of awareness and a deep sense of the contingent and indefinable nature of being. As he puts it in, Poem Half in the Manner of Li Ho: "We hang like clouds between heaven and earth, / between something and nothing, / Sometimes with shadows, sometimes without". (ibid: 89) A gentle irony infuses Wright's writing, as if he always reminds himself, and us, that whatever we say, or write, we can only hint at what is here at every moment in all its evanescent glory. In another poem he writes: "Open your mouth, you are lost, close your mouth, you are lost, / So the Buddhists say". (ibid: 53) The relational contingency of the universe can never be grasped by language and art, indeed it is the grasping that is the problem. Hence, as Wright reminds us, the Buddhists also say: "Live in the world unattached to the dust of the world". (ibid) But it is difficult to follow this advice, as Wright points out in very distinctive fashion:

> Not so easy to do when the thin, monotonous tick of the universe
> Painfully pries our lips apart,
> and dirties our tongues
> With soiled, incessant music.
> Not so easy to do when the right front tire blows out,
> Or the phone rings at 3 a.m.
> (ibid: 54)

The compulsion to speak so often overcomes the knowledge that silence may be best. Life continually intervenes to upset our plans and philosophical reflections. Wright's sense of the immanence of the divine in the everyday, is always counterbalanced by a playful sense of humour that leads him to avoid heavy-handedness in his treatment of metaphysical ideas. There is always a modest tentativeness – a *perhaps*, a sceptical *maybe* – in his writing that reminds us not to take any statement as being in any way definitive or certain. Like Montaigne, Wright seems to be a reluctant "believer", wary of institutionalised religion and its attempts to regulate our sense of the sacred. He believes "what the thunder and lightning have to say", and that he will "die like a cloud, beautiful, white, full of nothingness". (ibid: 156) For Wright, what is important seems to be *this* world, *this* life, not a transcendent realm beyond what is here. As he writes, "God is the fire my feet are held to" – an enigmatic remark that I interpret as suggesting that he stands on this earth and it is this place that is sacred, singeing us with its intensity. Wright sums up his position in a suitably laconic manner:

> I'll take as icon and testament
> The daytime metaphysics of the natural world,
> Sun on tie post, rock on rock.
> (ibid: 87)

In Wright's scheme of things, "nature" includes the human realm – the everyday unfolding of human imagination, aspiration and dissatisfaction – all of which he contemplates with warmth and a deep sense of kinship. For, as Wright articulates it, "whatever enlightenment there might be / Houses compassion and affection" (ibid: 99) – a belief that is reminiscent of the thinking of both the Buddha and Michel de Montaigne.

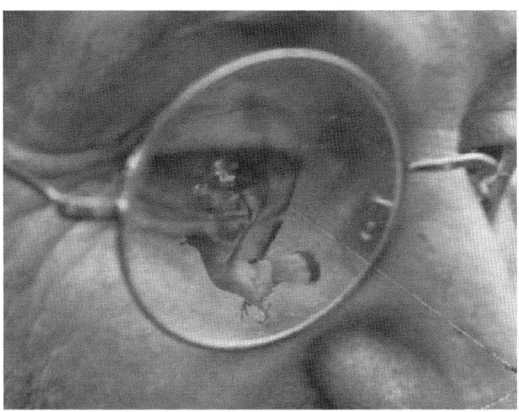

W.S. Merwin and August Kleinzahler

W.S. Merwin, the current American Poet Laureate, includes a poem titled, A Momentary Creed, in his recent collection, *The Shadow of Sirius*. (2009: 110) The title is indicative of Merwin's ambivalent attitude to the idea of a creed – a term which is usually used to denote *the* belief system to which an individual aspires or subscribes. In Merwin's case *a* "momentary creed", suggests that it may be one of many such creeds, which may change from time to time. The first stanza condenses Merwin's thinking into two brief lines: "I believe in the ordinary day / that is here at this moment and is me". (ibid) The poet identifies with the moment-by-moment unfolding of an "ordinary day" to such an extent that he considers it to be what he is and what he might become. However, the poet's field of awareness encompasses only a part of the whole spectrum of the present moment which "extends beyond whatever I may / think I know and all that is real to me". (ibid) Merwin accepts that "there is no place I know outside today", but immediately qualifies this assertion by adding, "except for the unknown all around me". (ibid) The "ordinary day" is not so ordinary after all, for it contains "everything that I call mine" but this "everything" is an act of grace and the poet acknowledges that even his belief in "the ordinary day" is a gift or rather a loan, a "momentary creed". (ibid)

August Kleinzahler, another contemporary American poet, engages with the quotidian in a way that echoes Merwin's "momentary creed", though he employs a very different vocabulary and manifests a very different sensibility. While Merwin's frame of reference is usually that of the natural world, ecological systems and Buddhist ideas, Kleinzahler's is the clash of urban and rural, popular culture and "high" culture – often delivered in a droll ironic tone that suggests a poetic persona that is both streetwise and widely-read. In, The Damselfly, a poem included in his collection, *Red Sauce, Whiskey and Snow*, (1995: 17) Kleinzahler opens with uncertainty as to whether what he is seeing is a "petal of jasmine caught up / by the breeze" or a "morning glory aflutter"? He then realises it is neither, "not a flower at all". It seems instead to be a butterfly and he goes on to describe its attributes with poetic precision. At this point, another voice comes to mind and he has to reconsider his position yet again: "*Ah*, the older poet tells me, /

that's a damselfly". This tale of mistaken identity continues with the words of "the older poet" admonishing Kleinzahler for his impatience and lack of observational acuity: *"And if you just slowed down / and looked, / you'd see all sorts of things"*. In a laconic, wry manner Kleinzahler suggests the importance of awareness, taking notice, taking care in perceiving what is going on as clearly as possible.

In another poem, Watching Dogwood Blossoms Fall in a Parking Lot off Route 46, (ibid: 71) we can see how Kleinzahler orchestrates his brief perception of natural beauty in an urban context alongside references to Tu Fu (or Du Fu), a Chinese poet of the Tang dynasty – a cultural leap that is surprising yet seeming to be entirely appropriate. Kleinzahler's dogwood blossoms aren't falling on a mountainside in a pristine wilderness but in a parking lot near "Phoenix Seafood / and the Savarin plant". The poet notices "this solitary tree and the last of its bloom" after he's been to the hospital to visit his mother, who sits with "the ashen old ladies / lost to TV reruns flickering overhead". As a counterpoint to this keenly observed image of old age Kleinzahler notices how the "adulterated, pearly light and bleak perfume / of benzene and exhaust" make the dogwood "as stirring somehow" as "that shower of peach blossoms Tu Fu watched / fall on the riverbank / from the shadows of the Jade Pavilion". Seen through the polluted light in the parking lot Kleinzahler experiences one of those passing epiphanies that happen when least expected. In this case, bringing to his mind the ancient poet, Tu Fu, who watched the peach blossoms fall and listened to the music of golden orioles – a music which somehow "found out the seam of him / and slowly cut along it". This idea, that something noticed can cut deep into the mind like a miner cutting along a seam of coal or gold, exemplifies Kleinzahler's distinctiveness as a poet, and reminds the reader of how moments of insight and realisation can arise within the flux of day-to-day living.

For Merwin and Kleinzahler there is nothing straightforward, let alone simple, about the experience of being here. Indeed, there is great mystery, complexity and uncertainty about what it is to be here, to be a thinking, feeling, perceiving organism – aware of only a small part of the whole relational field within which we exist. It seems that one role of the poet may be to interrogate and celebrate this complex state – to ask questions about the seemingly obvious condition in which we find ourselves from moment-to-moment. Yet, the poet does this in a provisional way, accepting that the process of enquiry is its own reward, opening up as it does further questions and possibilities. The syntactical and semantic field of the poem, like any artwork, is always shifting, changing and re-forming as it is encountered by each reader or viewer. The artwork or poem is an arena, or field of play, in which uncertainty and infinite possibility are vital attributes of the dynamics of encounter and interaction. In this regard the poet or artist can be seen as having concerns and methods not unlike a sceptic like Sextus Empiricus, or a Buddhist like Dogen or Hakuin, or a mystic like Thomas Merton.

John Cage and Arvo Pärt – a piano prepared and a bell sounded

On pages 54-56 I discussed different kinds of silence in relation to mysticism. In this section I'd like to extend this discussion into the field of music. Silence, or relative silence, is an integral component in any music. Used either as punctuation, or as part of the signifying substance of a particular work, relative silence enables us to distinguish between notes, chords and movements within the sequential development of each composition. In the work of John Cage and Arvo Pärt silence manifests itself, and is used, in two very different ways.

The American composer, John Cage, [see also p. 177 above] makes use of a kind of transparent silence, a silence that invites us to hear what else is going on in the soundscape around us. There is a porous quality to most of Cage's music which embraces the surrounding environment and draws our attention to everyday sounds and events that occur within the duration of a particular piece. Most famously, or notoriously, this openness is signalled in Cage's 1952 work, *4'33"* – which indicates the work's duration – four minutes, thirty-three seconds. The work is scored for a pianist whose role or performance consists of raising and lowering the lid of the piano to reveal and conceal the keys and to mark the three movements of the work. The audience is offered the opportunity to attend to the whole spectrum of sounds, (and sights and other phenomena), that happen to arise during this particular four minutes and thirty-three seconds. Cage provides us with a formal context in which to attend to what is happening all around and within us, all the time. As such, the work can be seen as a matter of taking notice, a disinterested paying attention, to the music of being – in all its contingency and informality. Cage lets in the light of the everyday, apparently non-musical, sphere, in order to show us what we often miss: the quotidian delights of everyday sensations and events.

While *4'33"* manifests transparent silence in a dramatic and controversial manner, many of Cage's works, throughout his career, also demonstrate the use of a similar transparency and openness. Early in his career, from the late thirties to the late forties, Cage earned a living as an accompanist to various dance groups and choreographers, writing music for an array of percussive instruments including found objects like tin-cans, kitchen paraphernalia and metal sheets. These were cheap and easily available and demonstrate Cage's inventiveness in practical and musical matters. All Cage needed were musicians to perform the works, but performers had to be paid and this presented Cage with a problem, as he earned hardly enough to support himself let alone others. It didn't take long before he found a radical and effective solution to this problem. Cage's father had been an inventor and Cage followed in his father's footsteps by inventing what he calls the "prepared piano". Cage was well aware that most of the halls in which dancers rehearsed had a piano as part of the furniture and by inserting various materials in between the piano strings (nails, bottle-tops, bits of felt, rubber, silver-paper, and so on) the usual sounds of the piano could be modified into a percussive orchestra within the one instrument. The prepared piano produces a range of sounds that are reminiscent of a *gamelan* – an ensemble of Balinese instruments, including many drums, xylophones and gongs. Cage, like his colleague, Lou Harrison, had an interest in *gamelan* music and its aural influence can be discerned in many works from the period.

While Cage's compositions for the prepared piano, don't display the theatrical shock-value of 4'33", they do make use of silence as both an important structural device and as a way of opening the music to the indeterminate sounds that occur while the music is being performed and listened to. In *Sonatas and Interludes for Prepared Piano*, written between 1946 and 1948, Cage weaves together a complex array of rhythmic patterns and short melodic phrases, but it is a very open weave. The various rhythms, irregular and regular, come and go as we listen to them, each one giving way to its successor like flurries of raindrops in a desultory shower or leaves falling from a copse of trees in autumn. There is no obvious melodic theme or rhythmic continuity holding each piece together. Although Cage is not making use of chance methods of composition at this time – that comes later, in the 1950s – he is making compositional structures that are short and seemingly fragmentary, broken by shorter and longer silences that give the whole work a quality of airy transparency. Each sound is given its own breathing space and we, the audience, can attend to each sound – savouring its distinctiveness and uniqueness – while being simultaneously aware of its relatedness to everything that goes on around it. Cage places as much emphasis on the gaps between sounds/notes as he does to the sounds themselves – the *Interludes* are, so-to-speak, as important as the *Sonatas*.

While Cage writes music of great porosity – full of gaps and silences that seem to let in the light, making use of diverse means and playful invention, the contemporary Estonian composer, Arvo Pärt, employs very pared-down materials and methods to produce music that is very condensed and apparently un-worldly – in the sense that it seems set apart from mundane everyday sounds and experiences. Indeed, while Cage displays no overt religious affiliations (though there are carefully considered philosophical and religious dimensions to his musical ideas), Pärt's work is made within a definite religious context, often making use of religious texts and liturgy. After growing up during the Soviet era in secular communist Estonia, Pärt became a member of the Russian Orthodox Church in the 1970s – though his interest in early Christian music, particularly Gregorian chant, had begun in the late sixties.

Despite the many pronounced differences in the music of Cage and Pärt, both composers have a particular interest in silence as a structural and signifying element. As we have seen Cage makes use of what can be called transparent silence, in Pärt's case the silence is more opaque. While Cage often uses relative silence to allow everyday sounds into the music, Pärt constructs silences that somehow keep us focused on the slowly developing textures and patterns of the work. In his early career Pärt wrote music rooted in twentieth-century modernism, particularly the use of serial techniques developed by Arnold Schoenberg and others. Following two prolonged periods of reflection and study, in which he produced very little work for public performance, Pärt returned to the concert hall in 1976 with music that was radically different to anything he had previously written. In a well-known statement Pärt describes the outcome of his studies (which had particularly focussed on church music of the fourteenth to sixteenth centuries) as follows:

> I have discovered that it is enough when a single note is beautifully played. This one note, or a silent beat, or a moment of silence, comforts me. I work with very few elements —with one voice, two voices. I build with primitive materials — with the triad, with one specific tonality. The three notes of a triad are like bells and that is why I call it tintinnabulation. (Anon. 2010c)

This statement can be interpreted as a musical *credo* and it has underpinned Pärt's music from the first performance of *Für Alina* in the Estonian capital Tallinn in 1976 to the present day. *Für Alina* is a short piano piece – the score is only two pages long, playable in two minutes – in the key of B minor, and is played very quietly almost throughout. The score contains a direction that it is to be played *"calm, exulted, listening to one's inner self"*. (Conen 1999) There is no time signature. The triad is a musical phrase of three notes – a particular note and its third and fifth above, for example: C-E-G. In *Für Alina* the triad is B, D (the minor third above B) and F# (the minor fifth above B).

Like Cage in the *Sonatas and Interludes for Prepared Piano* Pärt gives each note and phrase space to resonate, allowing the listener time to hear each distinct sound and cadence. Pärt opens out the architecture of his music so that we can clearly perceive each constituent part and each part is given equal attention. In *Für Alina* the performer is given room to develop the tempo as he or she thinks fit. The two melodic lines, a bass line and what sounds like a freely improvised upper voice, seem to be excerpts from an infinite score – each performer determining the duration and intonation of the work.

In the ECM recording of *Für Alina*, released in 1999, the pianist, Alexander Malter, spent several hours exploring the aural textures and dynamics of the work. Two phases of his extended exploration were included in the CD – each approximately 11 minutes in duration. One key element in Malter's realisation of the work is the central role of relative silence – the pauses between notes and phrases – an opaque silence in which the reverberations of a particular note are allowed to ring out like small bells, gently resonating in the aural spaces, lingering and dissolving before the next note is struck. This is a contemplative music, as much for the performer as for the listener, drawing attention to each nuance of sound and inviting us to perceive the music of being itself – being here in a space carefully listening. To refer back to my discussion of the many modes of silence [see p. 54] we might consider Pärt as manifesting in *Für Alina* the silence of the forest, *tishina*, the generative ground out of which sacred sounds, of God and human beings, arise.

Art and not-knowing

I'd like to end this chapter with some fragments of John Cage's writings re-orchestrated by me to give a flavour of his challenging thought:

> Our poetry now is the realisation that we possess nothing

> Out of a hat comes revelation & a pianist. On the way, she said she would play slowly. On the way she would play slowly. She said on the way she would play, play slowly. Everything, he said, is repetition. Slowly she would play. She would say playing slowly she hoped to avoid making mistakes, but there are no mistakes – only sounds, intended & unintended. A glass of brandy

> There are already so many sounds to listen to. Why then do we need to make music?

> We must work at looking with no judgement, nothing to say. All art has the signature of anonymity

> Art is a job that will keep us in a state of not knowing the answers

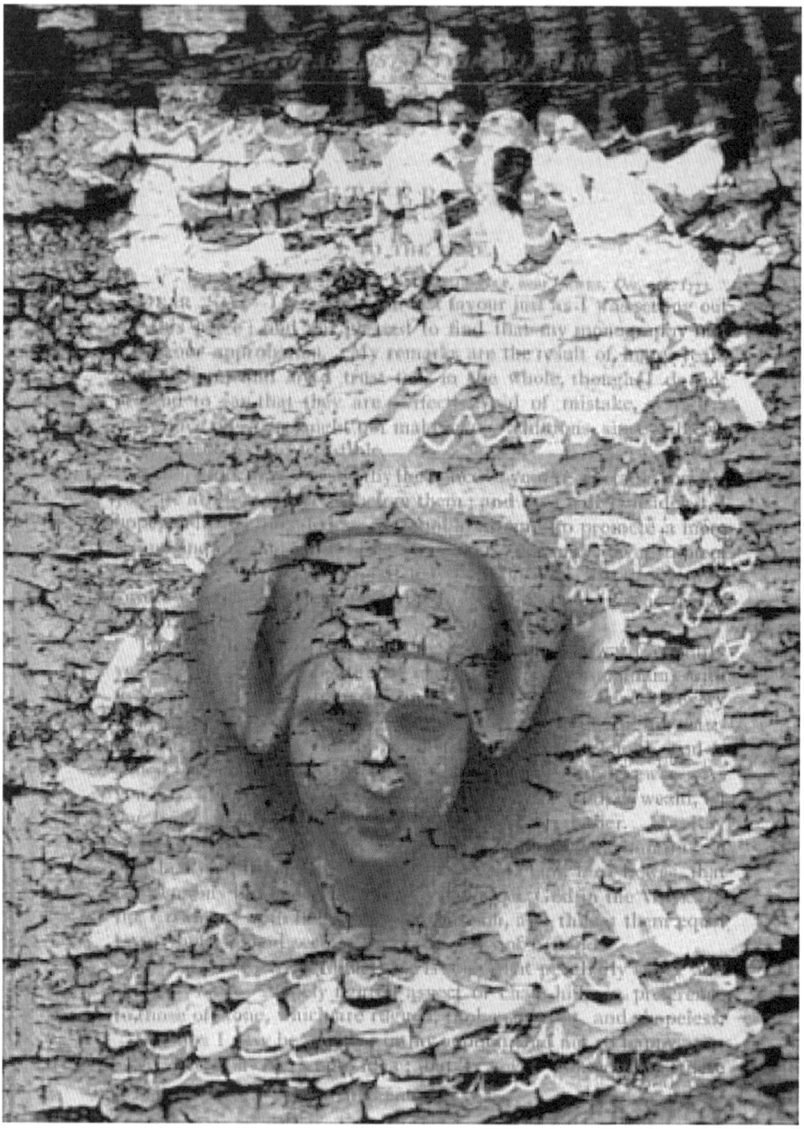

Part VII

A drawing together

> "No permanence is ours; we are a wave
> That flows to fit whatever form it finds:
> Through day or night, cathedral or cave
> We pass forever, craving form that binds.
>
> Mould after mould we fill and never rest,
> We find no home where joy or grief runs deep.
> We move, we are the everlasting guest".
>
> - from a poem written by the protagonist,
> Joseph Knecht, in Hermann Hesse's novel,
> The Glass Bead Game.
> (Hesse 2000: 407)

Drawing together

I have tried to show in these pages that mystics and sceptics are not fleeing from reality, or attempting to transcend it, but rather they are trying to engage with the world as it is, in all its contingent and relational uncertainty. They try to encounter the fluid, mutable and ungraspable actuality of the world as it constantly forms and re-forms around and through them. This world in flux can't be defined, categorised or pinned down. It is always slipping through our physical and intellectual fingers. The things of the world, which are really events, have no fixed form or identity, instead they have multiple and ever-changing forms and identities, arising from the constantly changing network of relationships which constitute the relational universe. And in this universe no thing/event has an independent existence, yet all things are unrepeatable instances – things/events are both unique and interdependent.

I have suggested that many mystics and sceptics, like many artists and poets are concerned with a never-ending experiential enquiry that involves a positive process of doubting and questioning – a process that can have no conclusions or final answers, as the subject of enquiry (living, being, consciousness) is always changing and reforming. This open enquiry into what it is to be alive necessitates a careful attending to the whole phenomenal field of which the person is an integral part. A balance has to be maintained between paying attention, being alive to being alive, and letting go, not clutching at or grasping at experiences, sensations and thoughts that come and go with great rapidity. Observing without commentary and judgement is not easy as it requires constant vigilance and the development of finely honed skills that can only come with practice and discipline.

To pay attention to the actuality of being here – being alive and present in this world – is to care, to pay heed, to take notice. There is an ethical dimension to this kind of non-judgemental contemplation which often leads mystics and sceptics to place value upon compassion, tolerance and respect for others. To experience life in all its contingency and mutability is to become aware that there can never be one absolute viewpoint, belief system or set of truths to which we must all subscribe in order to make sense of what we experience. On the contrary, careful scrutiny of the dynamic relational flux of being, tends to lead to a surprisingly firm belief in the need for multiple viewpoints, beliefs and truths, none of which can be considered as absolute or definitive.

The mystics, sceptics, poets and artists I've been discussing can be seen as offering alternatives to *dogmatism* – by which I mean an over-attachment to, or certainty about, particular beliefs or ideas which they consider to be true or absolute. Such dogmatism can be seen as a denial, or an attempt to ignore, the contingent, relational and mutable nature of existence – the uncertain, paradoxical and capricious nature of being. The writers and artists considered in these pages engage, with great clarity and realism, with a world that is uncertain and unpredictable, they consider this uncertainty and unpredictability as something positive – they realise that this is how things are, how we are. By recognising, accepting and working with the unpredictable flux of existence, these individuals transform uncertainty and contingency into opportunities for insight, understanding, equilibrium and play. They manifest wisdom, inventiveness and openness in their writings and artefacts, offering us examples of different ways of being, enquiring and doing – examples that we can learn from and develop in our own distinctive ways.

The mystics and sceptics I've been discussing tend to articulate a view of the universe as a dynamic multi-dimensional flux, made up of interdependent and interwoven networks of process and energy, a dynamic ever-changing matrix of chemical and biological structures – a field of forces more like an ocean or the Internet than a collection of separate *things* or objects. Indeed if the universe is viewed in this way there *can be no* separate objects with fixed essences or permanent boundaries, for every entity is transient and intimately related to whatever is happening in every direction around it.

Every transient form, including each of us, is a manifestation of the relational universe – a temporary gathering of qualities and attributes that are unique yet inseparable from the whole. When we refer to objects and beings as if they are separate and enduring, we need to keep in mind that this is a convention, useful for communicating and sharing knowledge and experience, but a convention nevertheless. The linguistic and symbolic systems developed by human beings over millennia provide us with tools of narrative and representation that enable us to analyse and reflect on our existence and to imagine alternative modes of existence, possible futures and fictions – but we have to keep reminding ourselves that such systems can lead us to reify, divide and categorise what is, in actuality, ineffable and unbounded.

If we exist as mutable structures within an ever-changing relational universe it may be useful to think of ourselves as permeable fields of possibility rather than as impermeable shells containing a kernel or ego that is a fixed repository of identity and selfhood – to think in terms of a relational self in a relational universe. Certainly many mystics and sceptics write about the self in this way. They consider the self as an evolving process rather than as a given object or idea – a temporary manifestation of existence that is a gift, a state of grace, and a matrix of possibilities. To be aware of the relational nature of the self, as an ever-changing manifestation of the relational universe, is also to realise that we are openings rather than closings, beginnings rather than endings. Mystics and sceptics suggest that we are open works, open to revision and transformation. We are creatures of curiosity & wonder – even if we temporarily forget that we are. Indeed artists, poets, mystics and sceptics, who are endlessly questioning, investigating and awakening to what is all around and in us, remind us that we *are* creatures of curiosity and wonder. And they remind us that there is no end to our explorations, no fixed conclusions to our enquiring, no permanent answers to our questions and therefore no fixed positions or beliefs to which we should become attached.

In a universe that is relative and ever-changing it is useful and perhaps necessary to realise that *we* are also relative and ever-changing, and that we may need to think of the *self* as an exploratory process of forming, shaping, making – an open-work in progress. We each have the capacity to take notice of our existence in all its contrary and contingent particulars and to re-form and revise ourselves from moment to moment. All organisms, including all human beings, have to find ways of negotiating the *contrarium* in which we find ourselves – finding ways to reconcile the irreconcilable, resolving the irresolvable – balancing the seesaw of possible courses of action.

The Buddha, like many mystics and sceptics, urges us not to assume that we are bound by habits of thought, feeling and action, but rather to realise that we always open to change – indeed we cannot avoid it. We are always growing and evolving. If we realise that we have no fixed essence and that the uncertainty of change provides us with endless possibilities for renewal we may become more at ease with the world and with ourselves. There is much we can learn from both mystics and sceptics about how to live in concordance with the contingencies and difficulties of being here. Both traditions (of mystical and sceptical enquiry) present us with ways of waking up to this life *as it is*, rather than as we might wish it to be.

I have tried to suggest in these pages that while there are many differences between mysticism and scepticism, there are also surprising similarities of aim and method articulated by many mystics and sceptics. Though they can be seen as coming from apparently opposite directions they do seem to meet and to share a sceptical non-attachment to many of the beliefs about the world and about ourselves which most of us take for granted. As agents of uncertainty, forever asking questions, they often achieve, as if by accident or grace, a state of equilibrium and peace of mind.

watching bird-thoughts fly

CODA

Zazen practice – a personal history

I have been involved in Zen practice for more than 40 years. I grew up in the Charnwood Forest area of Leicestershire in a small mining and quarrying village near to the appropriately named town, Coalville. In the mid-sixties in the town library I came across a copy of a text by Dogen, a thirteenth-century Japanese Zen master. Dogen is renowned as the most eminent writer and philosopher of the Soto school of Zen Buddhism – though I had no idea of this at the time. It is a mystery to me as to how this text, the *Fukan Zazengi*, probably in an introductory book on Buddhism, came to be in the library and how I happened to pick it off the shelves. Luckily Dogen's essay provides very clear instructions for *zazen* – sitting meditation – and I started to sit following Dogen's directions.

In the 1970's I developed my practice with advice from a Soto Zen centre in Northumberland and through various *sitting* groups. By the mid 1970's I'd established an informal Zen meeting place in Berkshire and for a while we were joined by an itinerant Soto Zen monk from Japan who was travelling through Europe. When we first met he complimented me on my *zazen* practice saying it was 'very strong' and he asked me who my teacher was. When I replied Dogen, he nearly fell off his meditation cushion. Perhaps because of my rather isolated introduction to Buddhism and the fact that I had to learn on my own – though I didn't feel alone as I had Dogen's words translated into clear and practical English – since this time I have had little involvement in professional Buddhist activities, developing my practice within the context of my daily life in a fruitful wilderness on the margins of institutionalised religion. The reader should take account of these factors when reading my comments. I speak with no authority other than my own experience.

To sit in *zazen* is very simple yet extremely difficult. It involves nothing more, or less, than sitting in full attention to the here and now – being-here – observing the mind in tranquillity without commenting or clinging to the experiences, thoughts, feelings and sensations that make up consciousness. When I look back to my childhood I realise that my earliest experience of this kind of mindful, undivided attention was as an animal watcher. I used to spend hours and hours out in the woods and heathland near my home, waiting for birds and animals to arrive at the place I'd chosen to sit – usually a rock, or a small clearing, or the foot of a tree.

I noticed that if I was agitated, or too hopeful, the birds and animals would notice me and keep their distance. But if I gave up any intention of being a bird-watcher, if I let go of my excitement, anticipation and hope, they would often wander right up to me – almost as if I wasn't there. And in a sense, *I* wasn't there. That is, the egocentric, unitary, 'I', wasn't there. Instead a different state of being was at work (or at play) – as if the edges of myself were dissolved into the surrounding space. It felt as if there was no separation between me and the world. As if the blackbirds, wrens, gorse linnets, and the occasional fox and badger that wandered by, were other essays in being, alternative manifestations of the life that flowed within me. It is this state

of being that *zazen* engenders and when I first practiced sitting meditation it felt very familiar, a return to the state of body-mind that I'd
sometimes experienced as a youngster sitting on a rock watching a
goldcrest only a few feet away making its carefully constructed nest.

For many years I followed very strictly Dogen's instructions in the
Fukan Zazengi – apart from the leg positions (I have never been able
to adopt the full lotus position, using instead a meditation stool). At
some point I adapted Dogen's guidelines to include a short period at
the beginning of each session in which I recite (to myself, not out
loud) what is known in Buddhism as The Three Refuges: I take refuge
in the Buddha, in the Dharma (the teachings) and in the Sangha (the
community of fellow Buddhists). I find that reciting this a few times is
a very effective way of focusing the mind. I've always used a version
of this chant in Pāli, the language of Theravāda Buddhism:

> *Buddham saranam gacchami.* (to the Buddha I go for refuge)
> *Dhammam saranam gacchami.* (to the Dharma I go for refuge)
> *Sangham saranam gacchami.* (to the Sangha I go for refuge)
> *Dutiyampi buddham saranam gacchami.* (For the second time I go to the
> Buddha for refuge – each phrase repeated)
> *Tatiyampi buddham saranam gacchami.* (For the third time - each phrase
> repeated)

I'm not sure where I first came across this melodious and gently
rhythmic version, but it has proved useful not only as a way of beginning *zazen*, but also as a way of calming my nerves before job interviews or dealing with other stressful situations.

If asked to describe "what happens" during my *sitting (zazen)* sessions
I would point out that each session, even after so many years, is very
different. Although a similar pattern may be evident, it is not always
so. Each time I sit I still feel as if I am just beginning and I'm never at
all sure what will happen. One thing I can say with relative certainty is
that in all these years I have very rarely finished *sitting* without feeling
more intensely alive, more at ease, temporarily wiser and often surprised. As to a pattern of what happens, I'll try to describe it: usually
when I begin there is a period, long or short, in which my mind flits
about from thought to thought, sensation to sensation; things then
begin to settle and to clear; sometimes the mental flitting-about reoc-

curs a few times, or a particularly persistent thought keeps returning, filling the field of attention for a while; but eventually, quite often, there's an opening of awareness, as if to the whole phenomenal field – as if the indeterminate stream of sounds, changing light, smells, thoughts, feelings, itches and flickering emotions are of equal value, pattering like raindrops on the windscreen of consciousness. Worries and hopes, joys and fears, are no more or less significant than the sound of a bird or the sensation of cool air on my skin. Everything seems alive and evanescent – a mutable universe of interwoven motions and events.

One pattern that often arises in *sitting* sessions is a move from having a clear sense of *myself* observing what is going on, an ego at the centre of *my* experience, a linguistic self spinning a web of words and thoughts, pouring out a stream of stories, commentaries, fantasies and what ifs – meta-narratives woven around the events and phenomena that arise from moment-to-moment – to a dissolving sense of self, a gradual letting-go of the control-tower self, watching the stories and commentaries dissipate until there is only an experience of thoughts, feelings and sensations arising, and no sense of a secondary self giving orders, commenting on, let alone owning, what is happening. It is as if this chattering ego self gives way, melts and becomes a porous, fluid succession of sensations, thoughts and feelings that *are* in process – a transparent lightened stream of selves emerging from moment-to-moment out of the constantly changing interactions of a relational universe.

Some of the most vivid moments of my life have taken place while sitting in this state of open awareness – or while walking or undertaking an activity in a *zazen* mode of consciousness. Certainly, however paradoxical it may seem, I have often felt most alive while apparently sitting still as a stone or doing something mundane like washing dishes or digging the garden. I have had euphoric joyous moments; periods of deepest tranquillity; feelings of indescribable connectedness with everything – as if I am dissolved into a great stream of intermingled possibilities; periods of intense clarity of mind; and feelings of kinship, empathy and compassion. But all of these states have come and gone and, in the end, *are of no particular significance*, compared to the moment-by-moment process of attending to their occurrence. It is the process of attending, being aware, being there as sensations arise and die away, without commenting on them (suspending judgement) or trying to hold on to them – it is this process which is, for me, the challenge, purpose and value of *zazen*.

On another level, for *sitting* involves both great simplicity and great complexity, this process can be seen as a letting-go, a casting-off of layers of accumulated verbal and mental silt, an unlearning of habits of thought and emotional response – an undoing as much as a doing. In this sense it is a vital counterpoint to the usual accretive, clinging, categorising activity of our minds. This may be why so often at the end of a period of sitting I have felt lighter, less burdened, suppler, ready to face what comes next in a slightly more flexible and robust way.

In my own practice I have tried to follow Dogen's guidance set out in the *Fukan Zazengi*. I suppose I see this as the bare bones of Soto Zen practice. Perhaps as a consequence of being for many years out in the wilderness, unconnected to any particular teacher or school, I have little interest in questions of lineage and transmission – matters which seem to be of importance to many Buddhist practitioners. No doubt I should take these things more seriously. However, as important as these concerns may be in ensuring that Buddhist practice remains somehow *true* to its historical roots, it may lead to a rather mechanical adherence to protocols and institutional formalities – with the danger that we can lose sight of the importance of the living quality of insight and practice manifested in individuals regardless of teacher, tradition or formal certification.

*

I sit here now thinking back to my time as an art student in Wales in the late sixties. I had already been doing *zazen* for a few years but in the first two years at art school I'd spent more and more time on my *sitting* bench. I would get up early to sit for a couple of hours and then do the same when I got home in the evenings. Sometimes the pain was intense, knees aching, bottom going numb. Most of the time there was the niggling to deal with. The niggling itches, the sneezing, the dry cough and the same ageing fly that seemed only to come alive when I sat on my bench. The fly seemed to have the patience of Job and the clinical insight of a surgeon as he chose all the places to land on my face, neck and arms that would cause me most irritation and distress. Behind my ears was bad, on my half-closed eyelids was worst of all. But he was a superb teacher. An insect guide to letting-go and letting-be. Without the fly I doubt I'd have learned so much from those long solitary hours. Slowly I'd learn to be unfazed by his buzzing. I'd feel his spiky feet moving over my skin and the urge to brush him away became less and less insistent. The glitter of his wings as he landed on the grey carpet became less and less magnetic to my vision. As the months went by I could hold my attention to the whole field of sight, sound and touch for longer and longer periods – until the fly became just one delight in the midst of many, one sensory motion in a shimmering field of sensations.

In the second winter, the hardest of the four I spent there, I sat most mornings next to an open window with a view down a long street of terraced houses rippling away to the docks. When I wasn't doing *za-zen* I could sit and watch the traffic, the tired cyclists and the pinched pedestrians clutching their coats as they walked against the biting wind. But when I was *sitting*, with the open window to my side or behind me, I could only see the pool of light dancing on the faded patterns of the grey carpet and feel the window as a slab of ice pulsating with menace reaching out with invisible fingers to every inch of my body. Looking back I wonder to what extent it was masochistic and self-indulgent. At the time I felt I was learning a great deal.

At first the cold was something to be fought against, to think about, slowly increasing in power and intensity as it became the centre of my attention. Somehow I couldn't escape its frozen tentacles. I was caught by my desire to be free of it. My mind became inflamed with strategies and ploys, arguments and counter-arguments, competing voices of advice, analysis and endless commentary. All of this only added to the force of the cold. As if I was packing more and more layers of ice on top of it, until I couldn't distinguish between my commentary and the silent ache of the cold. But everything I'd learnt from the fly came to my rescue. I drew on the patience he'd taught me and the methodical letting-go of each thought of pain and cold. Slowly but surely the chattering in my mind became just the chattering of my teeth. The cold became just another sensation, like the buzzing fly, a feeling amongst many – an icy slab beside a pool of grey, dimly-patterned carpet.

The cold and the fly taught me a lot about how to wake up to this life and about the discipline of art – probably more than I ever learnt from art school. They also taught me how to distinguish between the nip of frost and the nip, nip, nip of thinking about frost.

*

The practice of sitting in the way that Dogen advocates can be seen as both a mode of sceptical enquiry and as a way of waking up to the simple yet extraordinary fact of being here – a mode of attending to this life as advocated and practiced by many mystics. To sit in quiet and patient attention to the infinite particulars of everyday experience is not as easy as it sounds, indeed it can be extremely difficult. We have a tendency to construct endless commentaries *about* what is happening and what has happened within and around us, or we spend our time imagining what might happen or what we would like to happen. Either way we tend not to be present to this moment in anything other than a marginal way. It is as if our own existence, our being here, is of marginal interest, as if it is not worthy of clear unadorned observation.

To sit in this way, observing what goes on in and through us, it is necessary to set aside assumptions and habits of thought – for these tend to cloud and distort our vision. As we sit we begin to notice more and more, and we become aware of the glorious intertwining web of riches which we refer to as mind or consciousness. Our chattering, fantasising, desiring and regretting are integral to what we are, and although they have the power to entangle us in divisive and constricting patterns of thought, emotion and behaviour, they are part of our being – an aspect of our Buddha-nature or Buddha-mind. As such these qualities are not things that need to be scoured from our minds like stains on a teapot – as if they are failings or imperfections. Rather they are to be accepted, acknowledged and observed with care and benevolence – without clinging or additional commentary.

All our foibles, inconsistencies, doubts, dislikes and anxieties are material with which we can work – as much to be attended to as any other aspect of our being. Whatever comes into view has to be seen as important to the open-ended enquiry of *sitting*. It is important that we do not turn away from, or deny, aspects of our behaviour and do not pass judgement on them or label them as problematic, bad or unworthy. Rather it is by clear observance and non-judgemental noticing that we come to a realisation of who we are and how marvellous it is just to be here.

Triptych

I

everywhere and nowhere
 he is not, as much as he is,
  yet this stirring at the edges
   is where the world meets itself,
    inside meets outside, fusion of
    one with all,
                        to wake to this
             is to be in heaven while mired
             in earth's muddy glory

II

no thing is just a thing,
 for all things are sifted by light,
  stapled to each other, rivered
   through and through with what
   they are not as much as what
   they are, and so clouded
    they cannot be stunned or
     stunted by bounding line or
     definition
     whatever equation
      we invent to mark their place or
       mark their movement, the equation
        itself nudges them to an unpredictable
        somewhere else

III

no matter how long the list of
 qualities are ascribed to a speck of
  dust, there is always some remainder
   which, unlisted and unlistable, *is* the
    speck of dust

Bibliography

Abramovic, Marina. 1980. Rest Energy, video clip on YouTube. On line at: http://www.youtube.com/watch?v=3Tz-K4EC8hw (consulted: 25.10.2010).

Adorno, Theodor. 1973. *Negative Dialectics*. London: Routledge & Kegan Paul.

Annas, Julia. 2000. *Ancient Philosophy: A Very Short Introduction*. Oxford: Oxford University Press.

Anon. 2002a. *Shorter Oxford English Dictionary*. Oxford: Oxford University Press.

Anon. 2002b. 'Afterword', in *Tricycle* Spring 2002: 128.

Anon. 2010a. *New World Encyclopedia*. On line at http://www.newworld encyclopedia.org/entry/Syadvada (consulted: 20.03.2010).

Anon. 2010b. Wikipedia entry on Samuel Beckett. On line at http://en.wikipedia.org /wik i/Samuel_Beckett (consulted 27.10.2010).

Anon. 2010c. Singers.com entry on Arvo Pärt. On line at http://www.singers.com /composers/arvopart.html (consulted 17.11.2010).

Baas, Jacquelynn & Jacob, Mary Jane, eds. 2004. *Buddha Mind in Contemporary Art*. Berkeley & Los Angeles: University of California Press.

Baas, Jacquelynn. 2005. *Smile of the Buddha: Eastern Philosophy & Western Art from Monet to Today*, Berkeley & Los Angeles: University of California Press.

Bair, Deirdre. 1980. *Samuel Beckett: A Biography*. London: Macmillan.

Baker, B. & Henry, G. eds. 1999. *Merton and Sufism: The Untold Story – A Complete Compendium*. Louisville Kentucky, Fons Vitae.

Bakewell, Sarah. 2010. *How to Live: A Life of Montaigne in one question and twenty attempts at an answer*. London: Chatto & Windus.

Barthes, Roland. 2005. *The Neutral* (trans. Krauss, R.E. & Hollier, D.). N. York: Columbia University Press.

Batchelor, Stephen. 1990. *The Faith to Doubt: Glimpses of Buddhist Uncertainty*. Berkeley, California: Parallax Press.

Batchelor, Stephen. 2010. *Confession of a Buddhist Atheist*. New York: Spiegel & Grau.

Bate, Walter Jackson. 1978. *Samuel Johnson*. London: Chatto & Windus.

Beckett, Samuel. 1995. *The Complete Short Prose: 1929-1989*. New York: Grove Press.

Blaser, Robin. 1974. 'The Metaphysics of Light', in *The Capilano Review 6* (Fall): 35-62.

Blaser, Robin (ed.). 1975. *The Collected Books of Jack Spicer*. Los Angeles, USA: Black Sparrow Press.

Brutvan, Cheryl. 2008. *Antonio López García*. Boston, USA: Museum of Fine Arts Publications.

Burnet, J. 1971. *Early Greek Philosophy*. London: Adam & Charles Black.

Cage, John. 1966. *Silence*. Cambridge, Massachusetts & London: M.I.T. Press.

Cage, John. 1981. *For the Birds*. London and New York: Marion Boyars.

Capra, Fritjof. 2000. *The Tao of Physics*. Boston, USA: Shambhala Publications.

Caputo, John D. 1989. 'Mysticism and Transgression: Derrida and Meister Eckhart, in Silverman', H.J. ed. 1989. *Derrida and Deconstruction*, London: Routledge.

Caputo, John D. 1993. 'Heidegger and theology', in Guignon, Charles. B. (ed.) *The Cambridge Companion to Heidegger*. Cambridge: Cambridge University Press.

Carson, Anne. 2003. *If Not Winter: Fragments of Sappho*, London: Virago.

Carson, Anne. 2006. *Decreation*, London: Jonathan Cape.

Clampitt, Amy. 1998. *Collected Poems*. London: Faber and Faber.

Conen, Hermann. 1999. *White Light. Liner notes to CD: Arvo Pärt. 1999. Alina.* Munich: ECM.

Cranz, Edward. 2000. *Nicholas of Cusa and the Renaissance*. Hampshire, UK: Ashgate.

Creed, Martin. 2001. Selected writings by Martin Creed. On line at: http://www.martincreed.com/words/idontknow.html (consulted 22.10.2010).

Creed, Martin. 2010. Works: Work No. 227. On line at: http://www.martincreed.com/works/workno227.html (consulted 04.11.2010).

Cupitt, Don. 1998. *Mysticism after modernity*. London: Blackwell.

Danvers, John. 2006. *Picturing Mind: Paradox, Indeterminacy and Consciousness in Art & Poetry*. Amsterdam: Rodopi.

Davies, Oliver & Turner, Denys, eds. 2002. *Silence and the Word*. Cambridge: Cambridge University Press.

Dogen. 2009. *New World Encyclopedia*. On line at http://www.newworldencyclopedia.org/entry/Dogen (consulted 19.07.2010).

Dreyfus, Georges. 2003. *The Sound of Two Hands Clapping: The Education of a Tibetan Buddhist Monk*. Berkeley & Los Angeles: University of California Press.

Duncan, Robert. 2010. Poetry Foundation website. On line at http://www.poetryfoundation.org/bio/robert-duncan (consulted 01.11.2010).

Eagleton, Terry. 2008. 'Determinacy kills', *London Review of Books*, 19 June 2008, p. 9-10.

Eco, Umberto. 1989. *The Open Work*. Cambridge, Massachusetts: Harvard University Press.

Eliot, T.S. 1959. *Four Quartets*. London: Faber and Faber.

Empiricus, Sextus. 1990. *Outlines of Pyrrhonism* (trans. Bury, R.G.). New York: Prometheus Books.

Epstein, Mark. 2004. 'Sip my Ocean: Emptiness as Inspiration', in Bass, Jacquelynn & Jacob, Mary Jane, eds. 2004. *Buddha Mind in Contemporary Art*. Berkeley: University of California Press: 29-35.

Girbau, Basil. 2003. Disillusionment is positive. On line at http://www.hermitory.com/articles/interview.html (consulted 04.12.2003).

Hamill, Sam & Seaton, J.P. eds. 2007. *The Poetry of Zen*. Boston: Shambhala.

Happold, F.C. 1970. *Mysticism: A Study and an Anthology*. London: Penguin Books.

Harada, Sekkei. 1998. *The Essence of Zen: Dharma Talks Given in Europe and America*. Tokyo: Kodansha International.

Harmless, William. 2008. *Mystics*. New York: Oxford University Press.

Hartmann, Franz. 1891. *The Life and Doctrines of Jacob Boehme*. On line at http://www.sacred-texts.com/eso/ldjb/ldjb04.htm (consulted 12.02.2010).

Hecht, Anthony. 1998. *Collected Earlier Poems*. Oxford: Oxford University Press.

Hesse, Hermann. 2000. *The Glass Bead Game*. London: Vintage.

Izutsu, Toshihiko. 1984. *Sufism and Taoism: A Comparative Study of Key Philosophical Concepts*. Berkeley, USA: University of California Press.

Jacobson, Nolan Pliny. 1970. *Buddhism: The Religion of Analysis*. Illinois: Southern Illinois University Press/Arctus Books.

Johnson, Ronald. 1967. *The Book of the Green Man*. London: Longmans.

Kaplan, Abraham. 1962. *The New World of Philosophy*. London: Collins.

Kemp, Martin, ed. 2001. *Leonardo on Painting*. Yale, USA: Yale Nota Bene.

Kenner, Hugh. 1948. *Paradox in Chesterton*. London: Sheed & Ward.

Kessler, Michael & Sheppard, Christian, eds. 2004. *Mystics: Presence and Aporia*. Chicago: University of Chicago Press.

Kleinzahler, August. 1995. *Red Sauce, Whiskey and Snow*. London: Faber & Faber.

Kim, Hee-Jin. 1987. *Dōgen Kigen: Mystical Realist*. Tucson: University of Arizona Press.

Kim Hee-Jin. 2010. Dōtoku – Expression. On line at http://earlywomenmasters .net/shobogenzo/d/dotoku/dotoku_kim.html (consulted 31.03.2010).

Levertov, Denise. 1997. *The Stream and the Sapphire: Selected Poems on Religious Themes*. New York: New Directions.

Littlejohn, Ronnie. 2005. Daoist Philosophy, Internet Encyclopedia of Philosophy. On line at http://www.iep.utm.edu/daoism/#H4 (consulted 19.05.2010).

Low, Albert, ed. 2006. *Hakuin on Kensho: The Four Ways of Knowing*. Boston, Massachusetts: Shambhala.

MacCurdy, Edward, ed. 1956 A. *The Notebooks of Leonardo da Vinci* Vol. I, London: Jonathan Cape.

MacCurdy, Edward, ed. 1956 B. *The Notebooks of Leonardo da Vinci* Vol. II, London: Jonathan Cape.

Magee, Bryan. 1987. *The Great Philosophers: An Introduction to Western Philosophy*. London: BBC Books.

McEvilley, Thomas. 2002. *The Shape of Ancient Thought: Comparative Studies in Greek and Indian Philosophies*. New York: Allworth Press/School of Visual Arts.

McFarlane, Thomas J. 2004. 'Nicholas of Cusa and the Infinite'. On line at www.integralscience.org (consulted 06.06.2005).

McPherson, Conor. 2006. 'Chronicles of the Human Heart', *The Guardian*, 1 March 2006. On line at http://www.guardian.co.uk/ stage/2006/mar/01/theatre .beckettat100 (consulted 18.10.2010).

Melnyczuk, Askold. 1996. Beckett's Brightness on Dark Days. On line at http://www.samuel-beckett.net/boston/bright.html accessed 18/10/2010 (consulted 18.10.2010).

Merton, Thomas. 1967. *Mystics and Zen Masters*. New York: Dell Publishing.

Merton, Thomas. 1968. *Zen and the Birds of Appetite*. New York: New Directions.

Merton, Thomas. 1970. *The Wisdom of the Desert*. New York: New Directions.

Merton, Thomas. 1973. *Contemplative Prayer*. London: Darton, Longman & Todd.

Merton, Thomas. 1999. *The Other Side of the Mountain: The Journals of Thomas Merton*. Volume Seven 1967-1968. New York: Harper Collins.

Merwin, W.S. 2009. *The Shadow of Sirius*. Northumberland, UK: Bloodaxe Books.

Midgley, Mary. 2001. *Gaia: The Next Big Idea*. London: Demos.

Miura, Isshu, & Sasaki, Ruth Fuller. 1965. *The Zen Koan*. New York: Harcourt Brace Jovanovich.

Moeller, Hans-Georg. 2006. *The Philosophy of the Daodejing*. New York: Columbia University Press.

Montaigne, Michel de, trans. & ed. Screech, M. A. 1993. *An Apology for Raymond Sebond*. London: Penguin.

Murray, Paul. 1991. *T.S. Eliot and Mysticism: The Secret History of Four Quartets*, London: Macmillan.

Murti, T.V.R. 1980. *The Central Philosophy of Buddhism*. London: Unwin.

Nagel, Thomas. 1979. *Mortal Questions*. Cambridge, UK: Cambridge University Press.

Oliver, Mary. 2004. *Wild Geese: Selected Poems*. Northumberland, UK: Bloodaxe.

Penelhum, Terence. 1983. *Skepticism and Fideism*, in Burnyeat, Myles, ed. 1983. The Skeptical Tradition, Berkeley: University of California Press.

Perloff, Marjorie. 1996. *The Dance of the Intellect: Studies in the Poetry of the Pound Tradition*. Evanston, Illinois: Northwestern University Press.

Petersson, Robert, T. 1970. *The Art of Ecstasy: Saint Teresa, Bernini and Crashaw*. London: Routledge & Kegan Paul.

Phillips, Adam. 2005. Review of *William Empson, Vol.1: Among the Mandarins* by John Haffenden (Oxford: Oxford University Press) in The Observer (17 April 2005).

Phillips, D.Z. 1986. *R.S. Thomas: The Poet of the Hidden God*. London: Macmillan.

Rockefeller, Stephen C. 1989. *Nishitani and Dewey's Naturalistic Humanism*, in Unno, Taitetsu, ed. 1989. The Religious Philosophy of Nishitani Keiji, Berkeley: Asian Humanities Press.

Russell, Bertrand. 1946. *A History of Western Philosophy*. London: George Allen & Unwin.

Russell, Bertrand. 1963. *Mysticism and Logic*. London: George Allen & Unwin.

Schierz, Kai Uwe, et al. 2003. *Ineffable Beauty: Mystical Paradox in 20th Century Art*. Cologne, Germany: Salon Verlag.

Schneider, A. 1979. *Working with Beckett,* in Graver, L. & Federman, R., eds., 1979. Samuel Beckett: the Critical Heritage, Boston: Routledge, pp. 173-88.

Scott, Kirsty. 2005. 'In the Nature of Things: a profile of Kathleen Jamie, *Guardian Review* (18 June 2005).

Sells, Michael A. 1994. Mystical Languages of Unsaying. Chicago: University of Chicago Press.

Sextus Empiricus. 1990. *Outlines of Pyrrhonism*. New York: Prometheus Books.

Shusterman, Richard. 1993. Pragmatist Aesthetics: Living Beauty, Rethinking Art. Oxford: Blackwell.

Silverman, Hugh J., ed. 1989. *Derrida and Deconstruction*. London: Routledge.

Sinclair, Iain.1996. *Conductors of Chaos: a poetry anthology*. London: Picador.

Spiegelman, Willard. 2005. *How Poets See the World: The Art of Description in Contemporary Poetry*. New York: Oxford University Press.

Stryk, Lucien, & Ikemoto, Takashi. 1965. *Zen: Poems, Prayers, Sermons, Anecdotes, Interviews*. New York: Anchor Doubleday.

Tanahashi, Kazuaki, ed. 1995. *Moon in a dewdrop: writings of Zen master Dogen*. New York: North Point Press.

Teilhard de Chardin, Pierre. 2008. *The Phenomenon of Man*. New York: Harper Perennial.

Thomas, R.S. 2001. *Collected Poems: 1945-1990*. London: Phoenix Press.

Thomas, R.S. 2004. *Collected Later Poems: 1988-2000*. Northumberland: Bloodaxe Books.

Tomlinson, Charles. 1997. *Selected Poems: 1955-1997*. Oxford: Oxford University Press.

Turner, Denys. 1998. *The Darkness of God: Negativity in Christian Mysticism*. Cambridge, UK: Cambridge University Press.

Uchiyama, Kôshô. 1990. *The Zen Teaching of 'Homeless' Kôdô*. Kyoto: Kyoto Sôtô-Zen Center.

Viola, Bill. 1995. *Reasons for Knocking at an Empty House: Writings 1973-1994*. London: Thames & Hudson.

Walker, Susan, ed. 1987. *Speaking of Silence: Christians and Buddhists on the Contemplative Way*. New Jersey, USA: Paulist Press.

Watts, Alan. 1989. *The Way of Zen*. New York: Vintage Books.

Weeks, Andrew. 1991. *Boehme*. New York: State University of New York Press.

Weil, Simone, trans. Rees, Richard. 1970. *First and Last Notebooks*. Oxford: Oxford University Press.

Weil, Simone, trans. Crawford, Emma & von der Ruhr, Marion. 2002. *Gravity and Grace*. London: Routledge Classics.

Wolters, Clifton, ed. & trans. 1961. *The Cloud of Unknowing*. London: Penguin.

Wright, Charles. 2001. *Negative Blue: Selected Later Poems*. New York: Farrar, Straus and Giroux.

Zimmerman, Michael. 1993. 'Heidegger, Buddhism and deep ecology', in Guignon, Charles. B. (ed.), *The Cambridge Companion to Heidegger*. Cambridge: Cambridge University Press: 240-269.

Index